THE RIGHT WAY TO
PASS THE DRIVING THEORY
TEST

THE RIGHT WAY TO

PASS THE

DRIVING

THEORY TEST

Vic Marriott

RIGHT WAY

CONTENTS

DEDICATION

This book is dedicated to everyone who has given me a driving tip during all my years on the road. Ranging from John – my first driving instructor – my brother Roy and the late Matt Varty who taught me to drive large vehicles – to the gesticulating loonies who offer a totally different kind of initiative. I have included most of the good advice I was given, added to that my own experiences, and tried to spare you the rest.

INTRODUCTION

I only wish it were possible to put old heads on young shoulders, or to be able to give experience out in handfuls but, sadly, it is not. It has been a maxim of mine since I started teaching more than twenty years ago that, 'He who knows *how* will always have a job, but he who knows *why* will always be his boss'. I think the next best thing to trying to do the aforesaid impossibilities is to give as deep an understanding of the heart of the subject matter (hazard awareness) as possible, for that is what sound driving theory is all about.

With that in mind, I decided to produce this rigorous analysis of the Highway Code and the Driving Theory Test for those about to embark on the arduous and sometimes frightening task of learning to drive. Drivers who pass their driving Test join Britain's crowded and busy roads alone, having until then been protected by their driving instructor, and having had the benefit of the instructor's knowledge and experience on tap whenever tricky situations developed in front of the tuition car.

Once on your own, circumstances never seen before are bound to arise which will have to be dealt with in the cold light of day (and in the cold dark of night) without any help. Quite apart from the Driving Theory Test, that is why you need this book.

The Highway Code is the starting point because it sets out the rules of the road. My text relates to those rules the theoretical knowledge you need and widens out its scope wherever the Theory Test syllabus demands it. Though this book is slanted towards car drivers, motorcyclists and others should also be able to benefit from the material it covers.

Driver error is the common factor in most accidents. Statistics suggest that young drivers, particularly in the seventeen to twenty-one year old group (which makes up about 10% of British drivers) are responsible for about 20% of road accidents. The evidence points to young males being several times more at risk than young females. There is also research which leads to the conclusion that drivers in this age group take nearly twice as long to spot potential hazards as older motorists.

It's not just the carelessness or exuberance of youth that dominates the statistics. All new drivers, whatever their age, sex, abilities etc., need a chance to gain experience. For it is lack of experience, not confined to the young, which emerges as the overriding culprit.

Following an EC directive and in an effort to meet the challenges presented by immaturity and inexperience, the Department of Transport created the driving Theory Test.

The Theory Test takes the form of a multi-choice, written exam, comprising 35 questions. There are plans to replace the written exam with a computer-based method early in the new millennium. The Department of Transport have assembled a collection of over 1,000 questions. These have been grouped into exam batches, each paper having a range of up to 14 subjects and a combination of questions intended to present equal difficulty overall. There are special arrangements for those who cannot read or write, and translations available for foreign language speakers whose knowledge of English is insufficient for the standard Test.

Learners **can** start practical driving tuition before taking the Theory Test, though not all will choose to do so. You must hold a provisional driving licence before you can take the Theory Test. To gain your full driving licence both Tests must have been passed. Until then you must not drive unaccompanied.

At the end of the book, you will find a representative sampling of **ACTUAL** Theory Test questions drawn from the official Question Bank with the kind co-operation and copyright permission of HMSO and the Driving Standards Agency, executive agency of the Department of Transport. When you have read that far you should be able to answer 100% correctly! They are not there to learn by heart, but so that you can judge whether your knowledge is up to scratch. Trying them will demonstrate to you the precise level of understanding and knowledge required to pass the Theory Test.

Few would relish the pointless task of trying to memorise the entire 1,000 plus questions and answers in the official Question Bank. To know the answers without the knowledge required to use the information would be self-defeating. What this book does instead is to put at your fingertips a complete command of the principles upon which sound driving theory depends. Strongly linked to the rules of the Highway Code, the theoretical experience you will gain by studying the two together means you should be able to answer with confidence whatever selection of questions your Theory Test paper may throw at you.

Whilst the target of my book is Theory Test passes – through knowledge made easily digestible – I hope my book also proves to be enjoyable for other motoring enthusiasts who like to keep as up-to-date as possible.

In the interest of continuity I have restrained from him/her, his/hers, he/she and used the male term throughout. Ladies, please don't be offended by my political incorrectness!

1

OTHER ROAD USERS

If we were **all** fully aware of, and complied with, the road traffic rules, regulations and laws at all times, there would be an immediate reduction in the number of driving accidents. Overall stress levels would be reduced, and perhaps even good manners might come back into fashion. The Highway Code is designed to inform everyone who uses the highways of the rules; not just motorists, but pedestrians, cyclists, riders and people in charge of animals, etc.

It would be easier for each 'category' of road user to avoid difficulty with another, if he knew the rules to which they should be adhering. Most of us fit into at least two categories, e.g. 'motorist and pedestrian'; some of us fit into several, like 'motorist, pedestrian, cyclist and horse rider'. Those of us who know how another category *should* act in a situation are better equipped than those who do not. So, do not confine your reading of the Highway Code to just the bits for drivers. Go for a good understanding of the rules for all categories.

Hopefully, you will have read through the whole of the Highway Code (current version) at least once before you started to drive. If not, do it now! I suggest you keep your copy of it handy as you read my book, to enable you to double-check your complete understanding as I interpret for you.

Remember, wherever the Code says **MUST** or **MUST NOT**, it is telling you that this is to comply with the relevant law.

Pedestrians
The Highway Code gives pedestrians sound advice about how to get about as safely as possible. It tells them what they should expect from us motorists, in various situations. One very notable thing in this section is the lack of **MUST**s and **MUST NOT**s. Only two rules tell pedestrians they **MUST NOT**. This does tend to put the onus, as far as laws are concerned, on vehicle users. New

drivers seem to become better pedestrians. I put this down to realisation of how pedestrians affect traffic once we become part of it. However, it still surprises me how many of my pupils own up to not having read the pedestrian parts of the Highway Code!

If we know what to expect of pedestrians we should be able to minimise awkward situations and concentrate more on those which are out of the ordinary. However, pedestrians, ignorantly or deliberately, flout the rules on the spur of almost any moment. Haven't we all sometimes? Foolish or forgetful though any pedestrian may be, in the event of an accident the driver will invariably carry most or all of the blame in law. Being aware of errant pedestrian behaviour, and making allowances for it, are fundamental to good driving.

The Highway Code starts off by giving advice to pedestrians about using footpaths and how to walk safely when there is no pavement. It also mentions the wearing or carrying of *fluorescent* items in poor visibility and *reflective* items at night.

The Highway Code advises pedestrians when out with young children. Young children learn a great deal about how to respect the dangers involved with traffic from adults' behaviour. The realisation that this happens is necessary if adults are to avoid inadvertently teaching bad habits.

It also gives advice regarding groups or columns of pedestrians on the road. It details how the group should be lit at night and how to arrange look-outs at the front and rear etc., as well as repeating the fluorescent and reflective clothing details. At night, if you notice lights, or reflective objects swaying in the distance in front of you, it is probably someone on foot carrying a lantern, or maybe a light attached to a horse rider's boot. Always be prepared to slow down well in advance before you assess the safety of overtaking. Ramblers and soldiers are the most likely people to be found in groups on the open road, but the occasional protest march or organised charity procession is a more likely occurrence in town.

One of the pedestrian rules says they **MUST NOT** walk on motorways or their slip roads except in an emergency. Police videos of people walking on motorways have shown the disastrous effect this has on drivers. At the very least, it can distract their attention.

I remember once, stopping to render first aid at a major accident on the M1. It was late at night and pitch black. A vehicle had ended up blocking the two outside lanes with no lights on. I sent the next car driver ahead to the next emergency phone to get help organised;

however, another motorist ran back down the central reservation waving his white shirt in an effort to slow down traffic.

This caused mixed reactions. Most of the professionals – lorry, coach and van drivers – instantly recognise that someone on foot on the motorway means trouble ahead and reduce their speed and/or stop, putting on their hazard warning lights. Unfortunately, on this occasion, many of the other motorists looked at the chap running down the central reservation and thought 'He shouldn't be doing that'. By the time some of them looked back at the road ahead, it was too late for them to stop without hitting the rear end of those who had. What had started as one accident became quite a few. Fortunately, although there was a fair amount of vehicle damage, only one person was seriously hurt, and that was in the first collision.

Whilst I can appreciate that the running motorist was trying to help, he actually caused more trouble than he saved. The police reaction to him was mixed. 'Thank you for trying to help, but . . .'

Crossing the road

Most of us learned the Green Cross Code as youngsters, but do not be tempted to skip past the remainder of this section. It gives an amazing amount of information about how to cross the road safely, how the various different types of crossings operate and what pedestrians should expect drivers to do in given circumstances.

Quite early in my pupils' training we deal with crossings. I ask them how many different types of pedestrian crossing there are. It is surprising (even with those who boast of reading the Highway Code several times and fully understanding its content) how many do not mention Puffin Crossings. (Own up, how many of you just said 'What the heck is a Puffin Crossing?'?) Because they are traffic light controlled, most people group them with Pelican Crossings. It is important to note that (amongst other differences) you do not get a flashing amber light at a Puffin and therefore the procedure for setting off after stopping at one is different. You **MUST** wait for the green light.

The Highway Code gives advice to pedestrians about emergency vehicles, getting on and off buses, street works, and crossing rail or tramways. All of it is information which we, as drivers, need to recognise in order to deal safely with pedestrians involved in those situations.

2

THINGS MECHANICAL

If all of our vehicles were in a roadworthy condition (as called for by the law) that in itself would reduce the number of mechanical 'accidents'. You can suffer a very nasty incident if you hit debris, such as a silencer, dropped from another vehicle, especially if kicked up from under some other vehicle's wheels. With faulty brakes, steering or tyres you risk fundamental loss of vehicle control. Excessive play in the steering – when the front wheels don't respond almost instantly to steering wheel movement – needs to be investigated expertly and put right. An over or under-inflated tyre, for example, could make your vehicle slew to one side when you steer or brake. This could make the difference between having an accident or missing one. An incorrectly inflated tyre, as well as affecting your grip on the road, is also likely to wear out quicker because the tread will not be in even contact with the road surface.

To some extent you can identify faults yourself. Incorrect wheel alignment can result in your steering feeling heavy and in uneven wear across the tyre surface. With faulty, worn or poorly adjusted brakes you will notice they become less efficient, or they pull to one side. A simple test for worn shock absorbers is to press down sharply on each corner of the car and observe how quickly the car stops bouncing up and down. It should come to rest at once.

Incorrect wheel alignment, faulty brakes and suspension all affect the way tyres wear. If you suspect that your tyres, brakes, suspension, exhaust or steering are faulty, get them checked, and if necessary corrected, by a reputable garage. Many garages offer free or very reasonably priced checks on these items.

Tyre pressures should always be checked when the tyres are cold. I would suggest you check your tyres for correct pressure, obvious damage and wear on a daily or at least a weekly basis. Also give them a thorough check before you set out on any long journey. Remember the spare; that needs to be in a usable condition too.

Your tyres **MUST** have a minimum 1.6 mm of tread across the centre three quarters of their width all the way round each tyre. They should be inflated to the correct pressure and not have any cuts or lumps (carbuncles) on the tread or the walls. Remember to check the inside walls (the parts underneath the car) of your tyres too. They are no less vital for being out of sight. Also take care and drive reasonably after fitting new tyres. You should allow them to 'run in' (settle) for the first 100 miles.

Don't forget to check the level of your brake fluid too. If it needs to be topped-up on a regular basis, the lost fluid has to be going somewhere – probably somewhere it shouldn't – like over your brake pads. Similarly, keep an eye on your clutch fluid level.

Clear all-round vision (including the view in all your mirrors) is vital. If your front and rear screens (and side windows) are dirty, your chances of not seeing a driving situation developing put you in a very dangerous position. In law you could be in the wrong too. If you have got extensive scratches on your windscreen, night glare from other vehicles' headlights will make for poor visibility. Anything more than minor chips or cracks may render your screen liable to fail an MOT Test. Garages can check damage against the rules. If your windscreen wipers are worn or damaged, or your screen washer is faulty, get them replaced. This is fairly inexpensive and is also a requirement of the law. In winter your washer fluid may need an additive to prevent it freezing.

Remember, on the days when your vision is not clear, it is likely that other drivers' vision will not be clear either. If you cannot see clearly because of sun, fog, snow, or heavy rain, they will not be able to either. If one of you is not considering that fact, then **all** of you are in jeopardy.

Your interior mirror and the inside of your windows can get pretty dirty too, and should be cleaned on a regular basis. This will make a surprising difference to your all round vision. Whilst you have the cleaning materials handy, make sure that your dashboard instruments are clean as well.

Lights, reflectors, mirrors, windows and indicators **MUST** be clean and functioning properly. If they are not, you may be unable to see properly and/or you could give other road users the wrong impression of what your vehicle is and what it is doing. Imagine you are travelling along a narrow country road in the dark. You notice a headlight coming from the opposite direction. It is fairly well over to the other side of the road, which leads you to think 'there is a motorcycle coming the other way' and you keep your normal road position accordingly. The nasty surprise comes when you realise it is actually a tractor with only its nearside headlight working and towing a trailer that takes up more than half the road.

Headlights must be adjusted properly to illuminate the correct part of the road and prevent undue dazzle for other road users. A heavy weight in the back of your car (which will lift the front) can make even your dipped headlights a hazard to the driver of the vehicle in front. Take particular care not to dazzle him with your lights in his rear view mirrors.

Lack of a tail-light or stop-light is illegal and can be so distracting to some following drivers that they will go to amazing lengths to tell the offending motorist. I have seen people leap out when stopped at traffic lights in order to run to the car in front with such a message, only to find that they have not secured their own handbrake properly! The resulting accident, or embarrassment in avoiding same, has to be seen to be believed.

However, they do have a point. A broken stop-light means that those following may not realise when you are braking. It is not just the driver immediately behind you who needs to see your brake-lights. Picture yourself travelling in a stream of traffic. Consider the car in front of the one in front of yours. You will rarely be able to see both of his brake-lights at the same time. Well, what if the one you can see when he does his emergency stop is the broken light? The car in front of you is going to be braking hard without you getting any early warning from the car in front of him (i.e. the one with the broken brake-light).

This is where the other parts of this section of rules come into their own. I hope your seat belts are functioning correctly and your seat is firmly anchored to the floor etc. etc. I also hope the surfboard is securely fixed on the roof rack and the dog is behind his dog guard (and I hope that's fixed in properly too).

All loads **MUST** be secure and **MUST NOT** stick out danger-ously. If you have an object which overhangs the front or rear of your vehicle by more than two metres, you **MUST** secure a warning (such as a red rag) to the extreme end of it, in order to make others aware of the danger. Remember, added weight will affect your steering and braking etc.

It doesn't cost a great deal to buy some spare bulbs to carry in the car. It makes sense to carry a spare stop-and-tail bulb and a spare indicator bulb too. Make sure you are carrying the tools necessary to fit them.

The Highway Code also covers the same sort of information for motorcyclists, scooter and moped riders and their equipment. I put a lot of emphasis on being safe and being seen. It is all too easy for other motorists to 'not see' a two-wheeler, often with disastrous effect.

Your horn **MUST** be in working order. Make sure you use it considerately. It is *not* for expressing anger at other road users, but for informing them of your presence if you think they are unaware of you, and either jeopardising your vehicle or being endangered by it.

Incidentally, you **MUST NOT** sound your horn whilst your vehicle is stationary, except in an emergency (such as a vehicle reversing into yours). Also, you **MUST NOT** use your horn between 11.30 pm and 7.00 am in a built-up area.

Keep an eye on your engine emission levels. Smoke or excessive fumes indicate trouble which needs immediate professional attention to prevent pollution. Don't just await your next MOT Test or you can find your vehicle does not comply with the law. Engine oil and coolant levels (as well as the acid level in many batteries) need regular weekly checks. Coolant must include anti-freeze in winter. A seized-up engine or a failed battery can cause you immediate danger.

Roadworthiness of your vehicle is your responsibility at all times, not just when your vehicle becomes due for its MOT. If you are involved in an accident, or are stopped by the police, and your vehicle is found to be unsafe because you have not maintained it properly, your insurance cover could be declared void. This could render you liable to ruinous legal proceedings and/or make you financially responsible for any damage.

An important item not specifically mentioned in the Highway Code is the speedometer. This **MUST** be in working order. Without it, you will be unable to accurately monitor the speed of your vehicle.

Finally, make sure you are wearing appropriate clothing and footwear. These should enable you to maintain proper control of your vehicle, and not hinder you or your use of the controls in any way.

You will probably have been able to work out the philosophy by now. You can 'get away with' a lot, but only until the unexpected happens. When it does, you need all the help you can get. It is important to make sure you know the layout of the various controls and switches of the vehicle you are about to drive. All equipment needs to be in first-class condition and you need to be fully awake and aware at all times – which takes us neatly on to fitness to drive.

3

FITNESS MATTERS

It is a proven fact that our natural alertness wanes between the hours of midnight and 6 am, and it would obviously be best to avoid driving during those times, but there could well be other times when you may not feel, or be, fit to drive.

If you don't feel well enough to concentrate, don't drive. If you are simply too tired, don't drive. Find somewhere safe to stop (not on the hard shoulder of a motorway) and take a rest (fifteen minutes minimum after each 2 hours driving together with a short nap and/or cup of coffee, etc. would be ideal). About one in four motorway accidents are thought to be caused by drivers either falling asleep at the wheel or drifting into a sort of daze, by which time an accident is almost inevitable. Town driving is no different. You cannot afford to be drowsy. There are things to be concentrating on *all the time*. Always ensure there is fresh air circulating within the car.

Never drive while under the influence of medicines or drugs. Be careful with what you take. Even simple cough remedies can make you sleepy. If in doubt, ask the chemist, or your doctor if he is involved, whether you will be safe to drive whilst taking whatever you may need.

You **MUST** be able to read a car number plate from a distance of 20.5 metres (67 feet). If despite glasses or contact lenses (which **MUST** be worn if you need them) you cannot comply with this requirement, you shouldn't be driving. It is worth noting here that the Highway Code instructs that number plates should be kept clean.

I once had a pupil who did not realise his sight was poor until I asked him to read a number plate at the required distance. It was not vanity which had stopped him having his sight tested; he had just never noticed that his sight was so poor. He had been able to read books and newspapers, so he had assumed that his sight was up to scratch. Once he started wearing glasses, he told me he was noticing all sorts of things that he had been missing before.

You are allowed to wear sunglasses when necessary, but you should not wear them simply as a fashion accessory. The Highway Code warns against spray-on and other types of tinted windows. They may look smart but, after dark, they can seriously reduce the driver's vision. Reflection of the sun or another bright light in the mirrored glass type can cause blinding dazzle for other drivers.

I am going to assume that you are using a Department of Transport Approved Driving Instructor. This is not to say that mums, dads and friends cannot teach you to drive (provided that they are over 21 and have held a full licence for at least 3 years) but all ADIs have to be regularly checked by a Department of Transport ADI examiner to ensure that they keep up-to-date and are teaching you to the correct standard. Unfortunately, other people's bad habits can be passed on to you by a well-meaning parent or friend who does not know the current requirements of the DoT driving test etc. Often they will teach you to do something which is incorrect because they have been 'getting away with doing that' for years but as far as passing your driving Test is concerned, it is not up to scratch.

Having said all that, I acknowledge that some learners, for whatever reasons – lack of funds, time, or incentive – can't/don't take enough practice with an ADI before putting in for their driving test. This is where I feel parents can fill the gap. They can take learners out for practice sessions whenever it is convenient, and valuable experience on the road is the result.

The Highway Code is very clear on drinking and driving. So am I. **Don't drink and drive.** Take particular note of how very long alcohol stays potent in the body. I know a chap who went out and had a few drinks one night, then used a taxi to get home. Driving to work the next morning he had an accident, and was still over the limit when breathalysed at the scene. I can have just as much fun drinking soft drinks on an evening out as I would if I had some alcohol, but I realise not everyone feels the same. So, if you do drink, make sure you do not drive until the alcohol is completely out of your system.

Don't believe people who tell you that they drive better when they have had a couple of drinks. They **think** they do because their senses have been dulled by the drink. They feel more secure because they are artificially relaxed. The truth is that all the adverse effects listed in the Code have been proved in scientific tests. Though you have no way of measuring this for yourself, it is important to remember the legal limit for alcohol in the blood is currently 80 milligrams per 100 millilitres. The equivalent breath alcohol level is 35 micrograms in 100 millilitres of your breath. **ANY** alcohol in your system will adversely affect your concentration, co-ordination and the speed and accuracy of all your judgments. It will slow up your reactions and may cause misplaced confidence.

The rules and regulations regarding seat belts are explained well in the Code. Anyone who is not secured inside the car is not only in danger of being injured, but also of injuring other occupants of the car (including you, the driver) if they are flung about. The wearing of seat belts is compulsory for everyone unless one of the (very rare) exemptions applies, e.g. for medical reasons. It horrifies me when I see unsecured children in cars. It does not need much imagination to see them hitting the dashboard, or the back of the driver's or front seat passenger's head, or even going out through the front windscreen, in the event of a collision or emergency stop.

Remember, it is the driver's responsibility to ensure that children under 14 years of age comply with the law. If you are transporting tiny children, make sure they are secured in properly fitted safety seats. Where seat belts are fitted, older children and adult passengers **MUST** use them. Never allow children to travel behind the rear seats in a hatch-back or estate car.

Whilst considering the safety of children in the car, remember to use the child-locks on the back doors. These will make it impossible for them to be opened from inside by mistake. Also, make sure your head-restraints are positioned correctly. Not only can they minimise whip-lash neck injuries, but in the event of an accident, they might stop something/someone being thrown into you from behind.

The Rules about mobile telephones and other in-car apparatus are strict, and rightly so. You always need both hands and your undivided attention to control your vehicle. Even something as apparently innocent as unwrapping a sweet whilst driving will divert some of your concentration from the road. Anything which takes your eyes off the road or your hands away from the controls – for example, that sweet or putting a tape in the stereo – puts your safety at serious risk in the event of an emergency happening at the same time. Make a point of stopping in a safe place whenever you have to use a mobile phone, etc. Do not use them in petrol stations or at any accident where fuel or other inflammable liquid or vapour might explode or catch fire.

Finally, on this subject, remember that you **MUST** inform the Driver and Vehicle Licensing Agency (DVLA) about any health condition which is likely to affect your ability to drive.

4

BEHIND THE WHEEL

I will deal with Traffic Lights, Traffic Signs and Road Markings later in the book, but please note that the Highway Code says you **MUST** obey them as and when they give orders. That also applies if the signs or signals are of a temporary nature, such as at road works.

Attention! Signals

Your signals tell other road users what your intentions are, and their signals tell you theirs. However, just giving a signal does not give you the priority to act on it. Priority has to be given to you – not taken for granted. You should ensure that any signal you give is going to give the correct message. To do this your signal must be timed properly, executed in the correct place, and cancelled as soon as its message is no longer needed.

You should be prepared to react promptly to signals from others, but remain acutely aware that sometimes people give the wrong signal by mistake, and worse, sometimes change their minds without thought for the consequences. Consider that their speed and road positioning usually confirm their real intentions.

Many motorists do not seem to think it is necessary to signal if they cannot see another road user. An apparently simple manoeuvre like pulling up at the kerb, without a signal, becomes very dangerous if someone emerges from a driveway or side road just as you start to pull over. Not signalling a turn, because you cannot see another road user when you approach it, is not only dangerous if another vehicle appears in the turning, but also gives pedestrians no warning. Even in one-way systems you should signal every turn. Although the other motorists should know which way the traffic is flowing, some of the pedestrians may not.

You **MUST** obey signals given by police officers, traffic wardens and school crossing patrols. I also strongly advise that you obey signals being given by civilians – for example those who are helping to direct traffic around the scene of an accident or break-down. Any of the emergency services' personnel (ambulance, fire, police, etc.) may have occasion to direct or stop traffic, but they are not the only traffic controllers. Workmen at road works, burst water mains etc., often need your co-operation too. Also co-operate with signals from those in charge of animals – especially, for instance, if requested by a horse-rider to wait.

Moving off from the left-hand kerb. First, check both your rear view mirror and your driver's side mirror (I am assuming that you are driving a right-hand-drive car). Then signal. The Highway Code says 'if necessary', but in my experience it almost always is, so it's a good practice to do so every time. Don't forget to make sure the road ahead is clear too. You should also check over your right shoulder to make sure it is safe, because there is a blind spot there which is not covered by either of those mirrors. This blind spot check should be the last thing you do before moving off. If there is traffic approaching from behind you, you should not pull out, if to do so would make the other vehicles slow down, stop, or have to move over to avoid you. Be careful to time your signal to match with the gap you intend to pull into. Do not signal too early if there is a stream of traffic approaching from behind. This might make the drivers think you are going to push into the stream. Finally, remember to cancel your signal once it has served its purpose.

Moving on is very different from moving off. Moving on is what you do after you have stopped in a stream of traffic, or at traffic lights, etc. Before you move on, you should check your rear view mirror and **both** side mirrors. The danger here is of narrow or two-wheeled vehicles which are capable of squeezing in between you and the kerb, or between you and another queue of vehicles. Look out for them. Most times they will not be there, but the one time you forget to check will be the time you wish you had.

Correct positioning on the road not only helps to keep you safe, but also acts as an extra clue to other drivers of your intended route. As the Highway Code states, generally you should keep to the left unless road markings dictate otherwise for the route you wish to take. You **MUST** keep left whenever possible, and accept the basic principle that a driver on his own side (the left) of the road normally has precedence over others not so positioned. This is a good place to mention the amount of clearance you should give in the various situations you will come across on the road.

Positioning on the road and passing clearances
In the absence of any parked vehicles or other obstructions in the road, you should position your vehicle about one metre from the kerb. This will help you to avoid driving across drain covers etc. and allow you a bit of lee-way should a pedestrian step off the kerb. Should that occur or a pedestrian be pushed off the pavement (as sometimes happens in busy shopping areas) having that vital bit of clearance could save you from a nasty accident involving him, or a dangerous swerve into the path of oncoming traffic. At modest speeds, this metre should serve you well, but if a street or lane is too narrow to keep the clearance and remain within your own half of the road, you will have to slow down instead. At higher speeds (e.g. outside urban restrictions) a little more clearance is advisable, but if there isn't room to take a wider path, don't go so fast.

To pass a stationary vehicle or a row of them, you will need to have about one metre clearance. This positioning not only gains you that safety margin, it significantly improves your angle of view. It should improve your ability to react safely to a pedestrian crossing between cars, a driver walking round his vehicle in order to get in the off-side door, or even the idiot who opens an off-side door without making sure it is safe to do so.

When overtaking a bicycle, allow about one-and-a-half metres minimum. This extra clearance is for three main reasons. Firstly, cyclists tend to swing out suddenly in order to avoid riding across drain covers or through puddles, etc. Secondly, they wobble. Wind, rain, bumps in the road, or uneven loads – either in a back-pack or on their handlebars – can make their balancing act a bit more difficult than usual; or sometimes they may just be on the way home from the pub. This is not a joke. Although you could be breaking the law by being drunk-in-charge of a bicycle, you do not lose your driving licence for it. Thirdly, the slip-stream (air being pushed aside by a vehicle as it progresses) from a car can easily unseat a cyclist if you pass too close.

When passing horses, give them as much room as you safely can. Even if that means waiting for oncoming traffic until there is space to do so. Just as important as that space is the need to pass horses quietly. Any sudden noise might spook the horse and make it either difficult or impossible for the rider to manage. Don't be offended if the rider does not wave to thank you for your consideration, as he may be too busy keeping control of the horse. If horses are approaching from the opposite direction, or crossing the road in front of you, be prepared to slow right down or stop until they have passed.

If you have to squeeze through a narrow gap with vehicles one side and pedestrians on the other, try to allow the same amount of room (one metre) on *both* sides of your car. Otherwise a pedestrian stepping off the kerb or a carelessly opened door could become an accident of which *you* are a part cause, not having made sufficient allowance for predictable human error. If you cannot get that much room, be prepared to slow right down or even stop. Remember, there are certain types of vehicle where you should expect the doors to be opened immediately when they stop. A good example of this is taxis. Some taxi passengers do not even have a cursory glance to see if it is safe to open the door. Workbus passengers will often alight whilst the vehicle is held up in traffic, so keep a look out for them.

Finally, remember: there are no prizes for smacking mirrors off by passing too close to other vehicles. Depending on the make of car you are driving, the price of the mirror fitting, or even just the mirror glass, can be quite expensive. There is also the inconvenience and lack of safety involved until you can get the mirror replaced.

Generally, the correct road position should give you safe passage wherever you drive (provided your speed matches overall conditions appropriately), but sticking rigidly to a passing clearance of one metre from this and that, etc., does not necessarily always give you the best view of the road ahead. Remember these are minimum clearances. You may need more for safety in some circumstances. One thing is certain: you must relate your speed to the available clearance. Slow right down, even stop, whenever too small a gap requires it.

Consideration for others

You **MUST NOT** drive on a pavement or footpath except for access to property. It means that you cannot avoid a traffic hold-up by mounting the pavement, even if you only have to put your near-side wheels on the kerb. The dangers involved in so doing are not always obvious. No one would wish to run over pedestrians' feet, but you also have to think what damage may be done to the kerb stones (you must have seen one somewhere that has been rolled up onto its edge), the paving slabs, and even of the possibility of pavement collapse into basement areas. Most people on foot can see such damage and avoid coming to grief, but remember some pedestrians are blind – so think on.

The Highway Code instructs you to check your mirrors fre-quently so that you always know what is behind and to the sides of your vehicle. It also says that you should use your mirrors as part of your regular routine **well before** making a manoeuvre or changing speed. Motorcyclists are advised to physically glance behind them as well, to ensure it is safe before they act.

Whilst on the subject of mirrors, and with hazard awareness in mind, my routine instructions to pupils regarding when to use them might throw a little light on how to keep yourself informed about other road users' positioning and intentions.

You have three mirrors to use. The rear-view (interior) mirror, the driver's door (off-side) mirror and the passenger door (near-side) mirror. It is worth noting that the rear-view (inside) mirror is flat and gives an accurate distance perspective, whilst the door mirrors are made of convex glass which, whilst widening the view, do not reflect the true size and distance. You also have three basic driving plans each of which dictates the information you require to proceed safely.

Plan A – You are driving along a quiet stretch of road, with or without other vehicles following you. You have no intention to turn off that road and you cannot see anything ahead which will alter the situation. All you need do is check your rear-view and driver's door mirrors periodically (I suggest every five to eight seconds) to see if a vehicle has closed up on yours or has adopted an overtaking position. Make a point of checking again each time you have passed a junction to see if another vehicle has joined your stream of traffic, and each time you see a traffic sign, as this may initiate some action.

Plan B – You are aware that there is something ahead which might necessitate your slowing down. There can be many reasons for this and I suggest you keep the following list (as well as any others you care to add) in mind. Vehicles moving off from either kerb, traffic in front slowing down or signalling to turn, oncoming vehicles signalling to turn across your stream of traffic, pedestrians at the kerb or in the road, pedestrian crossings or traffic lights ahead, junctions ahead (where vehicles could emerge unexpect-edly), bends or narrow sections of road ahead, vehicles waiting in driveways for access to the road. The sight of anything in that list should prompt you to take an extra look in your rear-view mirror to establish who is where and what signals they will need should you have to take some action.

There are also situations which might make you have to move to your right. Stationary vehicles, cyclists, horse-riders and, where there is no footpath, walkers or joggers. To ascertain whether it would be safe to move to your right, it is (apart from your prime consideration of oncoming traffic) necessary to check your rear-view mirror first, then your driver's door mirror. Having moved out, you will need to check your rear-view and your near-side mirrors before you decide to move back to your left.

Remember, people *do make mistakes*; for example, they pull out foolishly late in front of you or even do so because they just did not see you, and so on. In many of the situations I have just listed you should be curbing your speed by easing off the accelerator anyway until you can see that the possibility of error can no longer affect you. If you do not reduce speed and make allowances properly like this, you will one day find yourself in an unnecessary accident because you were not in sufficient control to react in time. It is the first stage of braking that always takes the longest to achieve. If you are already preparing, and possibly even covering your brake pedal, you have a much better chance.

For Plan C, all or any part of the above could apply, because Plan C is adopted whenever you see something ahead which is definitely going to necessitate your stopping. You will need to decide (as in the following paragraph) about signalling, when and how hard to brake in order to stop in the correct place, and so on. Remember, the need to change from any one Plan to another can happen very quickly and the idea of having all the necessary information available to do this is a good one. (The mirror routines for turning come later in the book.)

The Highway Code also says to signal 'if necessary', in order to let other road users know your intentions. But how should you interpret 'if necessary'? An example of this could be on the approach to a pedestrian crossing. If you checked your mirrors and saw a vehicle fifty metres behind you, you might only have to ease off the accelerator in order to slow down sufficiently for someone to complete their crossing of the road. However, if the vehicle behind is much closer, say ten metres, then it would be much safer if you showed him your brake-lights early by a light touch on the pedal, to make him realise you are slowing and thereby make him start slowing down too.

The Highway Code advises you to keep a special look out for two-wheeled vehicles (motorcycles and bicycles) as they are particularly vulnerable in the event of an accident. This rule asks you to give them plenty of room, especially if you are driving a long vehicle or towing a trailer. Remember that two-wheelers can easily be hidden in your blind spots. Make a point of taking a minimum of two looks for bikes at junctions and roundabouts.

I once saw a coach, which had signalled a right turn (a bit late I might add), take a motorcycle round the turn with it. The motorcycle was already overtaking before the coach driver began his signal. Fortunately the rider was skilful enough to get round without having a collision with either the coach or the traffic island, but he could just as easily have ended up underneath the coach. The motorcyclist's comments were not suitable for inclusion here; however, why was he overtaking approaching a road junction . . .?

The Highway Code contains a rule designed to allow traffic which can travel at normal speeds to get past slower moving vehicles. If you are ever in the position of being the driver of a slow moving vehicle, try to remember how frustrating it can be to be stuck behind one. When it is safe to do so, pull in to allow other road users to pass.

Speed limits. I have gone into quite a lot of detail later in the book regarding what maximum limits are applied to different vehicles on all the different types of road. However, at this stage, please note you **MUST NOT** exceed any maximum speed limit which applies to you.

The Code also encourages you to recognise the extra danger and always drive slowly in residential areas. The increase in traffic calming measures is not without reason as I shall explain later.

The Highway Code points out that the existence of a speed limit does not necessarily mean it is safe to drive at that speed. Drive only as fast as the road, traffic and/or weather conditions dictate it is safe to do. You should drive carefully and more slowly if the weather conditions are likely to reduce the grip of your tyres on the road, for example when it is wet. Likewise you should drive slower and with extra care if visibility is bad, such as at night or in murky conditions where it would be particularly difficult to see cyclists and pedestrians. In fog, snow or on ice your speed must be cut back substantially further still.

Can you stop in time?
It is a rule-of-the-road that if you run into the vehicle in front or pile into the back of an accident, it will almost invariably be deemed **your fault**.

The Highway Code gives strong advice about keeping an adequate distance between you and the vehicle in front, in order to allow you to pull up safely if it suddenly slows down or stops. It shows a chart which gives the typical stopping distances (in metres, feet and car lengths) at speeds from 20 to 70 mph. Though car lengths are useful in giving you a visual image to use, the measurements in either feet or metres must be remembered too. It is those you may need to answer the relevant questions in your Theory Test.

The distances shown in the charts refer to dry, level road conditions, with good brakes, good tyres and an alert driver. Downhill gradients greatly increase your stopping distances. Tired or slow reactions, poor mechanics or slippery surfaces can dramatically extend those distances and anything that reduces the amount of grip your tyres have on the road will make it more likely that you could find yourself skidding.

As speeds rise, overall stopping distances multiply much, much faster: 70 mph is only 3½ times 20 mph, yet the overall stopping distance goes up 8 times! No wonder excessive speed, in the wrong places, *kills*.

At speeds up to 30 mph I recommend you keep a minimum distance of one foot for every mph between you and the vehicle in front. That will adequately cover the thinking distances shown in the Highway Code chart. (Happily the good old foot measurement keeps numerically in line with rising mph on the chart.) That means that at 30 mph you will maintain at least the length of two large estate cars clear in front of you. Provided you remain alert, and react immediately the vehicle in front shows his brake-lights, you should be able to stop before you collide with his rear end.

The theory is: at 30 mph the rear of his vehicle is 30 feet in front of you. When he starts to brake he will travel another 45 feet before he stops. You react as soon as his brake-lights show you he is slowing down. You start braking after 30 feet. You travel another 45 feet before you stop. You stop before the front of your vehicle hits the back of his. This should emphasise that the 30 feet clearance is a **minimum** distance. As the following driver, it is your responsibility to make sure you do not run into the vehicle in front.

All this theory mustn't lure you into a false sense of security just because you have assessed your gap correctly. You must be scanning way further ahead than the back of the vehicle immediately in front of yours. It is surprising how much information you can gain by looking around and ahead of the vehicle in front. It is often possible to be braking before it does.

Of course, you can only do this if it is possible to see further than the rear of the vehicle in front. When following a large vehicle which blocks that view (bus, lorry, refuse truck etc.) you must always stay back further so as to widen the extent of your vision. Remember, you are not just looking for other vehicles; pedestrians fare very badly in collisions. They can be seriously injured even in low-speed accidents. Any pedestrian struck at 40 mph or more will probably be killed. Take special care where pavements have been closed, or pedestrians redirected, due to road works.

Judging gaps becomes more difficult as your speed increases. The Highway Code suggests you keep a minimum gap of two seconds between you and the vehicle in front when on faster roads, but it does not tell you how to apply this. When you observe the vehicle in front of you passing a point where you could mark its position (e.g. passing a tree or road marking) start reciting this simple rhyme, 'Only a fool, breaks the two second rule' – a wording the Department of Transport suggest. If you pass the chosen marker point before you have finished saying it, then you are too close. You need to drop back and try it again until you make the gap correct. If another vehicle overtakes and pulls in front of you, re-establish a fresh two second gap behind him. From my many years of driving, and from what the 'experts' say, I believe there can be little doubt that driving too close and too fast for the road and traffic conditions is the cause of many accidents. Be warned . . .

Remember, this Highway Code rule *starts* by saying 'Drive at a speed that will allow you to stop well within the distance you can see to be clear.'

Finally, it also points out that you should at least double the distance if the road is wet and by even further if it is icy. Don't forget 'black ice'. It is invisible. You only realise you are driving on it when your steering mysteriously feels light, and the noise made by your tyres goes very quiet. When it is raining, your stopping distance could be doubled. When it is icy, your stopping distance could be up to ten times further than when it is dry.

It is a good idea to listen to traffic reports on your local radio station. Prick up your ears especially if they announce a diesel spillage. Diesel on the road surface should be treated like ice. It is most often spilt because the filler cap is not replaced after the tank is refilled, and usually happens as the vehicle (with full tank) navigates a corner or roundabout. Where better to have a skating rink than on a roundabout?!

All slippery surfaces will make your vehicle more likely to skid under braking or steering because the amount of grip between your tyres and the road is reduced. Some debris on the road, such as mud, leaves and grass cuttings, though not a great problem when dry, can cause savage skids when wet.

Loose surfaces, like sand, gravel and loose chippings (at road re-surfacing) also lengthen your stopping distance. This is partly why temporary speed limits are imposed after road re-surfacing until all the chippings have been embedded into the new surface. It is not only because the stones might be flicked up to damage windscreens and paint-work.

A bit less obvious are bumpy surfaces. If the road is bumpy, the weight of your car is momentarily lifted from the road as you reach the top of each bump, and is put back firmly as you go down after each one. If you have to stop quickly on such a surface, it is likely to reduce your grip and increase your stopping distance.

Extremely hot temperatures can soften the road surface, and this will lengthen your stopping distance too or affect your steering as well.

Another thing worth mentioning here is surface water. Sometimes there can be sufficient water lying on the road surface to create a mini bow-wave in front of your tyres. If you do not significantly reduce your speed by easing off the accelerator, it is possible for the water you are running over to lift your tyres clear of the road surface, leaving you with no grip at all. This is called 'aquaplaning'. You are left with no effective steering or braking in these circumstances, clearly something to be avoided. You only realise this is happening when your steering suddenly feels very light.

A word on braking skids

Remember, in a braking induced skid, you will travel further than you would have travelled if you had managed to achieve maximum braking (just before the wheels lock) without locking your wheels. This is what Anti-lock Braking Systems (ABS) do. Just as your wheels are about to stop turning, they adjust the pressure on the brakes, so that they maintain maximum braking without locking the wheels. Skidding may only add a few paces extra distance at low speeds, but that can mean the difference between stopping before you hit something (or someone), or just after.

The obvious remedy for skidding due to braking is not to brake so hard. The safest way to brake (which will also remove that nasty jolt at the end) is: brake gently, then harder as you begin to slow down, then ease off the brake pedal (not completely) just before your vehicle stops. In order to allow you to brake more softly, you will have to increase the distance between you and the vehicle in front. Remember also that braking less aggressively over a greater distance allows you to stop gently, as well as giving the following vehicle a longer warning (with your brake-lights) that you are slowing down. This in turn makes it less likely that you will be hit from behind.

On the subject of skidding, if you ever do get into a slide, turn your steering towards the direction your vehicle is sliding. If you are sliding to the right – turn to the right. Steering your wheels in the direction of the slide will help your tyres to regain their grip.

Basically, there are three causes for skids and slides. Braking too hard, steering too much or too quickly, and accelerating too hard. All three of these will make your tyres lose their grip on the road surface, and sometimes more than one of the causes could be involved in the same skid. The way to regain grip is by immediate removal of the cause of the skid and then **proper** use of the relevant controls.

If you are involved in a skid or slide but do nothing to rectify it, you risk your vehicle spinning. When travelling at high speed, a spin is inevitable if you do not immediately release your brakes when your rear wheels lock-up. The rear wheels lock-up first because hard braking throws the weight of the car towards the front end, making the rear tyres have less grip on the road. The light (and grip-less) end then tries to overtake the heavy end. Once in a spin it becomes harder and harder, and often impossible, to regain control.

Loosely related – if you are towing a caravan or trailer which starts to snake from side to side (there can be many reasons for this, such as unevenly distributed or shifting loads, punctures and high winds, etc.) do not slam your brakes on. Ease your speed off gradually until the trailer settles down again. Trailer snaking, for whatever reason, can be reduced to a large extent if your tow-bar set-up is fitted with stabilisers. Likewise, another useful safety item is a breakaway cable, which will apply the trailer's brakes if it becomes uncoupled from your vehicle.

If you suffer a puncture at speed, let the car slow down without braking at all if possible. Also, keep a firm hand on your steering. Slowing gently helps keep control in both of these circumstances, whereas hard braking would risk a violent skid or spin.

Brake Failure

Most modern cars have braking systems which are unlikely to let you down provided they are properly maintained. However, they will not tolerate over-abuse. Hard braking and continual use (such as relying on them to keep your speed down on long downhill stretches rather than changing down to a lower gear) will make them overheat, which in turn will make them work less effectively. A major cause of brake failure and brake fade is overheating: something to be avoided wherever possible.

Inclement and Winter weather

The Highway Code covers driving in foggy conditions so well that I strongly advise every driver to follow it to the letter. I do have a couple of useful tips to add to it though.

1. If you are waiting in position to turn right off a major road (and I trust continuing to signal your intentions) but have to wait close to the centre of the road for oncoming traffic to clear – keep your foot on the foot-brake. Your brake-lights then give even more warning to following drivers that you are stationary.

2. If you have difficulty deciding how fast it is safe to drive in poor visibility, remember the cardinal rule of stopping distances: you must be able to stop within the distance you can see is clear. Therefore, if you can only see for ten metres, you should be going slow enough to be able to stop inside ten metres.

You would be well advised to prepare your car for the winter conditions. It is particularly inconvenient and possibly dangerous to others as well as you if your vehicle breaks down because you have not taken these simple precautions.

The Highway Code mentions freezing or near freezing driving conditions and the extra care needed even if the roads have been gritted. The temperature can alter quite suddenly and I have seen places, particularly on steep hills, where a quick thaw can allow some melting snow to wash away the grit, just before it turns colder again and more snow and ice arrives. I suggest you frequently test your brakes, very gently, to establish the state of the road surface whenever you have any doubt about the amount of grip available.

You are also advised not to drive in snow unless your journey is essential. The Highway Code recommends that you use higher gears than normal at slow speeds to avoid wheel spin. Try not to do anything suddenly on snow or ice. Steering, braking, or accelerating too hard or quickly will almost certainly put you in jeopardy on snow or ice. Remember you **MUST** use headlights (normally on dipped beam) when visibility is seriously reduced.

If you have to travel a lot in snowy or icy conditions, it may prove to be worth investing in the appropriate special tyres for your type of vehicle. You **MUST** ensure that your windows, mirrors and all lights and indicators are clean and clear. Also, if there is any danger that you might be stranded by heavy snow falls, equip your vehicle with a shovel, some blankets, and perhaps even a flask of hot drink and some high energy food. Although the rescue services advise that it is usually best to stay with your vehicle if you are snowed in, it is obviously a good idea to have some warm clothing available in the car. Don't forget the boots and gloves. You may not like driving whilst wearing gloves, but having your hands suffer can be worse. Keep your fuel tank topped up. You could be in mortal danger if you cannot keep your vehicle heater running for any length of time whilst stuck in a snow drift. If you intend to carry extra fuel for just such an occasion – remember to use an approved container, not an old drink bottle. Take a hat too. A vast amount of your body heat is lost through the top of your head if it is left uncovered in the cold.

Having a tow rope aboard to help or be helped back onto the road in the event of a minor slip off the beaten track (always provided the vehicle is not too badly damaged) could save you a lot of delay and expense waiting for an already busy tow-truck.

Listen to local travel bulletins. These may help you to avoid the worst affected areas, or cancel an excessively risky journey which you might not be able to complete. Finally, much as I advise against using them whilst you are driving (it is illegal unless they have hands-free operation) a mobile phone can be a comfort if you do get stuck. Apart from it allowing you to call for assistance, your family or friends can get awfully worried if you do not arrive at the time they expect you.

5

PEDESTRIANS

The Highway Code deals with the driver's responsibility towards pedestrians. It is quite comprehensive and I do not intend to go right through it. However, it does not mention pedestrians who are deliberately awkward. Those who will cross in front of you very slowly (despite the Highway Code telling them they **MUST NOT** loiter on crossings), with the intention of rousing your anger. Sometimes they stop in front of cars, or even double back the way they came just as you are starting to drive off. Sometimes they may be alone, but most often they are showing off to their companions. Think what you like, but do not rise to the bait. It is no use retaliating by either sounding your horn, shouting or revving your engine at them. This is the reaction they are looking for and will only give them (in their eyes at least) an excuse to verbally (or even physically) assault you and/or damage your vehicle. Wait patiently for them to complete their crossing; it's your only sensible option.

Even more frightening are kids who 'compete' to be the last to dash across in front of your car. It is baffling to try to understand why they do it, but it is still your responsibility to avoid running into them. The Courts will always expect the driver to be able to stop in time.

Pedestrian Crossings. At Zebra Crossings (those with black and white lines across the road and flashing orange beacons) it points out that you **MUST** give way when someone has moved onto the crossing. I would like to include parents with prams and push-chairs, as well as people with dogs, in the list given of people for whom you should look out. Please be extra vigilant when pedestrians are carrying white sticks, as this signifies that they are blind. If you see they are carrying a white stick with red banding below the handle, this tells you they are both deaf and blind. Most of those listed will wait on the pavement rather than actually step onto the crossing, until they are *sure* you are going to stop for them. On the other hand, there are also some children (and some awkward adults) who are just as likely to step or dash out without giving you ample time to stop, so watch out for them too.

I adopt the attitude that crossings belong to pedestrians. I am always prepared to stop. I do not wait until I just happen to notice someone at or near a crossing; I actively look out for them as soon as I know there is a crossing ahead. If I can see that it is unnecessary to stop, then I accept this as a bonus and continue smoothly. The alternative to this attitude would make having to stop at crossings a nuisance and would only lead to stress and bad driving.

The Highway Code says you **MUST NOT** overtake or park in the confines of a pedestrian crossing (within the area marked by the zig-zag lines) but it does not explain why. It is quite logical really. If a vehicle is parked in that area, it will wholly or partially block the view of approaching motorists. Likewise, if you overtake within that area, the vehicle you are overtaking will be obscuring your view of the crossing. The restriction also applies in the area marked with zig-zag lines after you have passed over the crossing. Parking or overtaking there could mask the view of the crossing for drivers approaching from the opposite direction. It follows that you should **never** contemplate reversing round a corner or doing a turn in the road within the zig-zags. 'Overtake', incidentally, is carefully defined in Law for these rules. You cannot go past (either side of) any moving vehicle within the zig-zags nor past the leading vehicle that may have stopped for pedestrians.

I have taken the trouble to explain all this, as it seems a lot of experienced drivers do not think it is dangerous to overtake, park or manoeuvre there.

In a queue of traffic you **MUST** keep pedestrian crossings clear. That means do not stop in a position where your vehicle is either completely or partially on the crossing. If you do stop on the crossing, the pedestrians will not know whether to walk in front or behind you. They will not be sure if you are going to remain where you are, or will try to move forward or backward to clear the crossing. Always wait before the crossing until you can drive beyond it in one move.

Remember, you cannot control the actions of other drivers or road users, so do not make the pedestrians' decisions for them. At any crossing, Zebra, Pelican, Toucan or Puffin, *never* beckon pedestrians across. If you do, and another vehicle collides with them, they will blame you. They must decide for themselves when it is safe. At Toucans and/or cycle-only traffic light controlled crossings cyclists are entitled to ride across; again, it is for them to decide when so to do, not for you to encourage them.

The Highway Code tells you how the lights should control drivers' actions at a Pelican Crossing, and warns that a crossing with an island in the middle of the road **MUST** be treated as one crossing as long as it goes across the road in a straight line.

It helps if you pair up the light signals given to drivers, with those given to the pedestrians:

1) When we (drivers) have a green light, they (pedestrians) have the red man and should not cross.

2) When we have the solid amber light, we should be stopping because the next light will be the red one. At this time they have still got the red man.

3) When we get the red light to stop they, after a slight delay for safety, get the steady green man and may now cross. There may also be an audible beeping signal to assist visually impaired pedestrians.

4) After a time, which is set for each crossing, the green man starts to flash. This tells the pedestrians that, if they are already crossing the road – they should continue to the other side. But, if they have not yet started to cross – they should wait and press the control button to start the sequence again.

5) Whilst the green man is flashing, we have the flashing amber light. This means we **MUST** give way to pedestrians already on the crossing but, if the road is clear, we may drive on.

6) Finally, they get the red man again, and we get the green light. Remember, the green light does *not* necessarily mean go. It means if the crossing is clear and the situation is otherwise safe, then you can go.

Be on the look out for pedestrians who disobey the instructions given by the lights. Some will start to cross whilst the green man is flashing or even when the red man is showing. Never assume that if there is no-one standing beside a Pelican Crossing, the lights are not going to change against you. A pedestrian may have pressed the control button, but found an opportunity to cross before getting the appropriate signal. Sometimes youngsters press the button and walk (or skateboard) away, with no intention of using the crossing at all. At a Pelican, this will start the sequence which stops the traffic.

If the stop signal is showing, even when the crossing is empty – you **MUST** stop until the amber light starts to flash and the road ahead is safe.

Puffin and Toucan Crossings, though operated by traffic lights, do not have the same sequence as a Pelican Crossing. At no time does the driver get a flashing amber light and he **MUST** wait for the green light before deciding if it is safe to proceed. However, as a Puffin or Toucan Crossing uses sensors, in order to ascertain whether someone is waiting to cross or not, you are less likely to be stopped at an empty one.

6

ON THE ROAD

Emergency vehicles: Police, ambulance and fire service vehicles – along with bomb disposal, blood transfusion, mountain rescue and coastguard vehicles – are equipped with blue flashing lights and sirens; sometimes red flashing lights are used. A doctor on an emergency call is entitled to use a flashing green light. The Highway Code tells you to keep a look out and to listen for such vehicles. It asks you to make room for them to get past, but not to endanger others whilst doing so. I remember seeing some young men in a car with its windows shut. The stereo volume was so loud that their ear drums must have been touching in the middle of their skulls, and they were oblivious to the ambulance which was stuck a few cars behind them. They were delaying the flow of traffic by driving slowly and too far from the kerb. The thing that surprises me about this rule is that there is not a **MUST** or **MUST NOT** in sight.

I suggest that the way to give emergency vehicles maximum priority is to imagine their journey is going to end at *your home*.

The Highway Code suggests you drive carefully when you see a flashing amber light, because it warns of a slow moving vehicle. Any vehicle on the road which cannot exceed 25 mph is supposed to have a single flashing amber light to warn you of this fact. In certain circumstances even invalid carriages are required to have one.

Hazard Warning Lights

If your vehicle has broken down and is causing an obstruction, or needs to have attention drawn to it, switch on your hazard warning lights. Hazard warning lights are meant to show the vehicle is stationary.

The prime purpose of hazard warning lights is to highlight the fact that you have had to stop where you are causing an obstruction. Note the 'had to' (i.e. because of a breakdown etc.). They are not provided so that you can choose to stop anywhere you fancy and flaunt the rules.

Do not use your hazard warning lights if you are towing or being towed. In cases where they are used on the move, they confuse other road users. Other drivers do not know when you are going to turn, because your indicators are being used as hazard lights. There is also the danger that the driver of a vehicle, approaching another with its hazard lights on, will assume it is stationary when, in fact, it is on the move, and what looked safe is not.

There is one exception which allows use of hazard lights on the move. You can display them briefly whilst slowing down if you are joining the tail end of a stationary queue or coming to a stop at the scene of an accident **on a motorway or dual carriageway**. This warns following drivers that you are about to stop in a place where they would not normally expect stationary vehicles. It's best to switch them off as soon as another vehicle has stopped behind yours. This eliminates the possibility that you will drive with them on once the obstruction is cleared.

The Highway Code tells you how the police will give you the instruction to stop from their car. It should also be mentioned that a police officer can stop you from a motorcycle or whilst on foot. Remember, you **MUST** stop if a police officer instructs you to. Likewise, you **MUST** stop if a traffic warden or school crossing patrol instructs you to.

The Highway Code asks you to give way to buses whenever you can do so safely. I sympathise with bus drivers (I used to be one). I know they have to try to keep to a schedule and that passengers and traffic make their job specially difficult and stressful. I just wish some bus drivers would realise that the majority of other drivers would let them out at bus stops if it were safe at the time. However, some erring bus drivers appear to think the Code says you must always let them out. Consequently they often pull out when it is far from safe. Keep a look out for them. This rule also reminds you that people, hidden from view, are likely to be either rushing to the bus stop, or crossing the road from behind the bus. Look out for them too.

Drivers of large vehicles like buses and lorries have a much better view of the road ahead than we do. When you see them letting other vehicles go first despite their own priority, don't be cross. Their aim is almost certainly to help the overall flow of the traffic to your ultimate benefit as much as to others. Indeed, you should follow their example when you can.

The rules are quite clear about the way you should proceed when near horses. You should give them as much clearance as possible, even if that means waiting behind them until there is plenty of room, and then going past as quietly as you can.

The Highway Code puts priorities in perspective for single-track roads. In addition, if you retain a mental note of where the passing places are, as you go along, you will be better able to co-operate should the need to back up arise. The same trick can be employed when driving down narrow streets with parked vehicles on both sides. Once you have entered the narrow section, if there are no gaps, the only way out forwards is at the other end. The same will apply to any traffic coming from the other direction. So, have a good look through, before you enter. Always try and meet other vehicles in a wide part of the road, rather than to try to squeeze past where it is narrow. Take care not to assume everyone will give way when they should. Some drivers (either through ignorance or by mistake) will push their way through regardless of priority.

Lines and Lanes

Hazard warning lines are there to help you 'read the road'. They give important warning, yet few drivers appear even to notice when a centre line (fig 2) changes into a hazard warning (fig 1), or vice versa. Fig 1 and fig 2 show the difference between the two types. You can find them at the back of the Highway Code too.

Fig 1   Fig 2

The more observant drivers scan well ahead for these changes constantly. They know that every switch to hazard lines heralds danger and for good reason. They therefore moderate their speed unless or until the purpose of the change becomes clear and they can best judge how to proceed. To the uninitiated it seems uncanny how they always seem to know what's coming up, whether it's the brow of a hill, a bend, another road meeting or crossing their own or whatever. Once you're tuned in to the system you will discover it applies on motorways, approaching roundabouts and to all sorts of hazards.

Quite logically there are usually five hazard warning lines leading up to a Give-Way or Stop line. Sometimes there are more, but usually five. These can be useful in another way. I teach my pupils to slow right down to second gear speed, by the time they reach the first hazard warning line. This enables them to stop smoothly at the junction if necessary, or prepare to drive on gently in second gear if they assess it to be safe. Obviously, if it is a Stop line rather than a Give-Way line across the junction, they stop, but the hazard lines help to get them to the Stop line position smoothly.

Fig 3

Double white lines along the road in Britain are either **both** continuous, or one side or other takes the form of a broken line. The Highway Code tells you what you can or cannot do if (as you drive normally on the left) the nearest of double white lines is continuous as in either diagram in fig 3. You **MUST NOT** cross or straddle that continuous line unless you are turning into or out of a property or side road, or to avoid something stationary which is blocking your lane. If necessary, but only when it is safe, you may cross it in order to avoid an accident or in circumstances outside your control. You are also permitted to pass a road maintenance vehicle, a pedal cycle, or a horse, provided they are not exceeding ten miles an hour, and you may also cross the line to comply with police or traffic warden directions.

Remember, if you park on either side of a road with double white lines down the centre you will be causing a dangerous obstruction which, of course, you **MUST NOT** do.

When the nearest of the double white lines is a broken line (see fig 4) you are allowed to cross the lines to overtake, provided it is safe to do so. You must be certain you can complete your overtaking

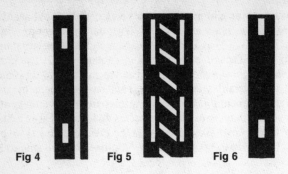

Fig 4   Fig 5   Fig 6

manoeuvre safely and in time to get back to your own side of the road before the broken line on your side reverts to a continuous one. Quite often, you will notice arrows in the centre of the road, curved in such a way as to direct you back to the left. These are designed to alert you to the fact that you need to get back to your own side of the road, because an unbroken line, bend or other hazard is ahead.

The Highway Code describes hatch markings (see fig 5) which are most often used in the centre of the road to keep streams of traffic apart. They are designed to protect things, such as traffic islands, vehicles waiting to turn right, and so on. You **MUST NOT** enter these markings if the surrounding edge line is continuous on your side, except in an emergency or in one of the other circumstances explained earlier above. The Code does allow you to enter the markings if the surrounding line is broken and you can see that it would be safe to do so, but I always recommend against this unless you have to pass something which is travelling very slowly (horse, road sweeper, etc.).

A chevron design may be used instead of plain, diagonal hatching within the protected area: the same rules then apply if the perimeter line on your side is a broken one; however, if that edge line is *continuous*, you **MUST NOT** enter the chevroned area in any circumstances other than in emergency. Such chevrons, however, are most often used to segregate driving lanes, for which purpose they are always enclosed on both sides by continuous white lines: examples include where a slip road lane (or lanes) meets with or parts from the lefthand lane of a dual carriageway or motorway, or where such roads themselves merge or diverge; clearly, you **MUST NOT** enter these chevroned areas from whichever side of them you may be.

Short broken lines which divide the road into lanes (see fig 6): wherever well-spaced short dashes clearly mark your carriageway into lanes, keep to the middle of your lane unless you need to change lanes; then use your mirrors, signal etc., as necessary.

The Highway Code also mentions the coloured reflective studs (cats' eyes) which are used to mark out the road. On single carriageway roads, white studs will mark the centre of the road and any lanes. On country roads there might also be black and white banded posts with red reflectors on your left and white on your right to help show narrow sections and the shape of sharp bends.

On dual carriageways and motorways, four different coloured studs are used. I think the most logical way to remember where each colour is located is to list them from left to right. Red studs mark the left-hand edge of the carriageway, with green studs across entrances, exits and lay-bys. White studs separate the lanes and amber studs mark the central reservation on your right. Knowing – without having to think twice – where each of the colours is located is essential when you are driving in thick fog in order to ensure you are in the correct lane. They are also extremely helpful when driving in the dark, particularly on unfamiliar roads.

There is often an additional white line, running along the left-hand side of the road. This line is to show you where the edge of the road is. It proves to be very useful when driving along a country road in the dark, or in fog. It can also help you find the way in to a property, because the solid line changes into a broken one across entrances etc.

Another useful additional to this set of lines is the 'rumble strip'. These are usually to the extreme left (and sometimes the extreme right) on dual carriageways or motorways. They are designed to make a distinctive grumbly noise if you touch them with your tyres. This noise should make you realise that you are running off the edge of the available road, and make you take some action before your vehicle leaves the road altogether. These rumble strips can also be found marking the edges of lanes where normal traffic should not cross over, such as bus lanes.

Extra, temporary, reflective, yellow studs may often be found at major road works where lanes have to be shifted about.

Lane Discipline
When there is an extra, 'crawler', lane you will find the slower movers, such as loaded heavy goods vehicles, using it to avoid holding up faster vehicles. If you feel the need to use this lane, remember that most of the vehicles already in it are probably struggling to keep their momentum up the hill. Try not to impede

them. Whereas you might have to change down one gear in order to keep going up a steep incline, they sometimes have to change down several if the traffic in front of them slows up. So, unless you anticipate having to slow down as much as the vehicles which need to use the crawler lane, try not to use it.

Fig 7

Many a dangerous situation or accident is caused by drivers drifting into, and not realising that they need not be travelling in the crawler lane, until they are trapped in between the real slow movers. They cause great difficulties to the faster moving vehicles when they try to regain the normal inside lane. Scanning ahead when you see the advance crawler lane warning sign shown in fig 7 (or perhaps merely one for a steep up-hill ahead – sign 73, page 113) should enable you to stay in the correct lane and avoid having to change lanes later.

A situation which is perhaps worse tends to follow when you should have seen the unfortunately somewhat insignificant-looking sign which says 'Slow lorries for X miles' on the plate below it. This sign is not even featured in the Highway Code yet it is *very* important. It is usually found on the hard shoulder of a motorway or dual carriageway. A red triangle encloses a white background with a picture silhouetted in black of a medium-sized lorry climbing a hill.

Perhaps because the large scale of the type of road on which this sign is normally placed reduces the visual impact of the land contours, and because it is placed a long way ahead of the problem itself, the significance of this sign often seems to fail to have any impact on the observer. Yet the trunk dual carriageway or motorway on which you are driving will have started rising towards a long, uphill gradient. It is almost inevitable that lorries are going to slow right down in the left-hand lane and that faster vehicles are going to want to pull out to overtake. A secondary, equally inevitable, result will then be that middle lane drivers will suddenly want to shift to the outside lane.

If any of them act without due care, faster traffic already passing is going to be in jeopardy. (They ought to have predicted the trouble and slowed down but invariably have not done so . . .) The scene is set for the savage, nose-to-tail pile-up in which we all fear ever being involved. Make sure you are never a guilty party in that scene.

The Highway Code says if you need to change lane, use your mirrors to ensure that you will not make another vehicle take evasive action, then signal before you move over. I am a firm believer in having a look over the appropriate shoulder as well, after checking the mirrors, in order to check the bit of road that the mirrors do not cover (the blind spot) and I am pleased to see that the Highway Code now recommends it too. Ninety-nine times out of one hundred the blind spot is clear, but just now and then there is a vehicle there and by doing the extra check I avoid a nasty situation. If you make the blind spot check a normal part of pulling out/moving to another lane, both to the right and left, the odd occasion when there is a vehicle there will make it worth while. Personally, I consider it an essential check.

I will always remember an incident when the extra check saved my life. I was driving along the M25 at 70 mph in the left-hand lane. There was not much traffic (remarkable in itself on the M25). As I approached an entry slip road, I was catching up with a slow moving vehicle. I decided that as soon as we had both passed the slip road, I would overtake if it remained safe to do so.

The slip road was one of those which brings you downhill onto the motorway, and some drivers use them like a chute to get their entry speed up to 70 mph (or – illegally – more) quickly. With this in mind, I scanned to my left as I drove alongside it. There was nothing in sight.

As I passed the end of the slip road, I looked in my left door mirror. There was no vehicle to be seen. My rear view (interior) mirror-check confirmed there was no-one closer than half a mile behind. I then checked my right-hand door mirror. The overtaking lanes were both clear for at least half a mile. I put on my right indicator and allowed it to flash twice before my customary blind spot check, *prior* to starting to move out.

As I turned my head to check the blind spot, a sports car zapped past, practically skimming the paint on my right-hand side at, I would guess, over 120 mph.

I can only deduce that during my left door mirror check up on the slip road, he had not yet entered it. Whilst I was looking in my rear view (centre) mirror, he must have been in my left door mirror. And when I was checking my right door mirror, he must have been hurtling up behind me in my rear view mirror.

This was an extremely worrying incident. I know that I have good peripheral vision. I notice things which are happening to the sides at the same time as observing things in front of me (an essential ability if you are to survive as a driving instructor!) but I did not notice the approach of this sports car. Thank goodness I make it a standard practice to check my blind spot before pulling out. I urge all my pupils (and you) to do the same.

On a carriageway with 3 lanes (or more) another danger is now commonplace if you are moving out to a centre lane, or returning there from an overtaking lane. You not only need to know that the lane you are going to move into is clear, but that no other vehicle is moving into it from the other side.

If another driver transfers from the other side into the same space that you do, you will meet like a pair of cymbals. It's a bad mistake, frequently triggering a much bigger smash as others (too close as usual) pile into the accident from behind.

You are well advised to follow direction signs as you approach junctions and get into the correct lane for your destination. Try to get into your lane early. Do not wait until the last moment before nipping across, as this could well cause problems for others who have already positioned their vehicle correctly, and whose safe driving you could jeopardise.

In unfamiliar territory you must therefore become skilled at observing direction signs, so as to select your correct lane. When you fail to do this, as we all do sometimes, remember you must not barge into the correct lane and cause other drivers to take avoiding action. Nor is it always safe merely to stop where you are until someone lets you in; doing that unexpectedly is a great way to get hit from behind. More to the point, you will hold up traffic behind you. Courtesy demands that you consider them first. Often the reasonable course of action is to abandon your intended route and drive on in the lane you are in; then find your way back to your route without inconvenience to others.

Be patient. Do not try to queue-jump by switching lanes. Though it may seem like a good idea at the time, the amount of time you save is so minimal as to make the extra risks taken not worth the trouble. I once conducted an experiment, with me driving courte-ously and within the speed limits, whilst another driver deliberately tried to get to our destination as quickly as possible. Whenever possible he travelled at 40 mph, in a 30 mph limit. He swapped lanes in order to get into the shortest queue wherever traffic was stopped at traffic signals or in general hold-ups, whilst I tried to drive like a chauffeur transporting a lapful of volatile explosives with a very sensitive fuse. After a ten minute journey, during which I felt quite relaxed, whilst **he** had one anxious eye out for the police, we arrived within a few seconds of each other.

I think it is worth mentioning here, that smooth orderly progress, with moderate – never fierce – acceleration, correct use of your gears and gentle operation of your brakes will reduce both the amount of fuel you use and wear of your brake pads. Whilst on the subject of using less fuel – though different engines will produce slightly different results – generally speaking, driving at 70 mph uses approximately 30% more fuel than driving at 50 mph. (Worth remembering if you are not really pressed for time on a journey.) Driving smoothly also reduces the amount of exhaust gases (pollution) your vehicle releases into the atmosphere and therefore makes you a more environmentally friendly driver.

Lane discipline: try to follow these rules to the letter as they impose restrictions on the use of certain lanes. This will, in the long run, save the embarrassment of being caught in the wrong lane. In the wrong lane, depending on the circumstances, you could find yourself missing turnings, having to go round one-way systems for a second time, or holding up other traffic and having some irate motorist flashing his lights at you from behind. Incidentally, flashing your headlights or hooting at someone from behind either tends to make them deliberately hinder your progress, or panics them into other errors in an effort to get out of your way. Neither option makes for safe driving.

Notice how these rules expressly define circumstances in which certain lanes should not be used.

The Highway Code specifically encourages you to return to the left lane after overtaking on dual carriageway roads. Sometimes however, on dual carriageways, it is necessary to overtake a number of vehicles in one manoeuvre. I use a simple rule to decide whether it is appropriate to pull back into the left lane between two vehicles if a particular gap is quite short. I estimate whether I will reach the next vehicle that will need to be overtaken in 15 seconds or less. If it will take longer to catch up with it, then I start planning to pull back in. If not – I stay out in the overtaking lane provided I am not thereby holding up faster-moving traffic.

Do not travel in an overtaking dual carriageway lane if the lane to your left is clear. It is most annoying for following vehicles. Likewise, if you have a slower vehicle in front of you which is blocking the overtaking lane, and there is no available overtaking lane to your right, do not flash your headlights. As has just been explained this may be interpreted as aggressive behaviour and can even provoke an aggressive response.

A practice which seems to be quite acceptable on continental dual carriageways is, when slower vehicles are hindering your progress, to drive at a safe distance behind (2 seconds back) and put on the appropriate direction indicator to show you want to pass. When the driver of the slower vehicle notices your indicator, he is much more likely to move over for you. However, the idea must not be used where the presence of junctions could mean your signal being misinterpreted in any way.

Road Rage

I could probably write a whole book about this subject but, for the purpose of this book, I will limit my comments to the following.

Many things cause road rage, some of them so simple as to be unbelievable. Overtaking dangerously and/or cutting in are easy examples, but simple things like blocking the entrance or exit to a side road whilst queued up on the main road, playing an in-car stereo system too loud, or throwing rubbish out of the car windows can cause other road users to lose their cool.

Firstly, don't be the one who offends. Be considerate at all times. Do unto others as you (and the law) would like you to be done by.

Secondly, don't get involved. If someone behaving badly affects you, remember that (unless you are a policeman) it is not your responsibility to put him (or her) straight. If you can, without endangering yourself or others, note the relevant details, then by all means report the matter to the police, but even doing that is sometimes not worth the hassle involved.

Thirdly, keep yourself safe. Remember that losing your temper will move your concentration away from the perspective it should have – driving correctly – and that in turn may make you behave like the unreasonable, irrational moron who upset you in the first place. Ease off if some idiot cuts you up or pushes in front, swaps lanes, gesticulates, flashes his lights or blasts his horn at you. Don't let your driving skills be reduced by the foolish (albeit dangerous) actions of others. Remain calm and keep control of both your vehicle and your temper. If you find that you have been unable to accept dished-out abuse without losing your concentration, etc., find somewhere safe to pull over and stay there until you have regained your own composure, before you drive on.

7

OVERTAKING

Overtaking is probably the most perilous part of normal driving. Unless completed properly, unnecessary dangers are involved but these can be minimised if you follow a routine which ensures the safety of both yourself and other road users.

The Highway Code describes the procedure which should be followed when overtaking. It reminds you of the Mirrors-Signal-Manoeuvre sequence. Don't forget to check the blind spots, which are not covered by your mirrors, as well. Remember, if another vehicle is about to pass yours – do not start your overtaking sequence. You do not want the other driver to think you are going to pull out on him. Therefore do not signal yet, until he has passed you (or clearly decided not to). Also ensure you have engaged a suitable gear to allow you enough acceleration to complete your overtake quickly.

The Highway Code covers the overtake from the moment you signal and will subsequently move out if it remains safe. If you find, on having moved out, that you then cannot get straight past, make sure you never sit in the other vehicle's blind spot. If necessary, signal and get back into the lane you have just left, provided you can do so safely. This rule also tells you to get back to the left after you have overtaken, but not to cut in front of the vehicle you have just passed. In order to give that vehicle sufficient space, I make it a rule (on dual carriageways and motorways) not to move back to the left, until I have the whole front of that vehicle in my rear view mirror and I have also checked the near-side door mirror and blind spot.

On single-carriageway roads, extra care is needed to ensure there is sufficient clear road ahead to pass before you need to get back over to the left. Before you start your overtaking manoeuvre, you must consider traffic approaching from the opposite direction, traffic islands, bends in the road ahead, dead ground* and road

---

* *Dead ground is that part of the road ahead which you cannot see when the road is like a switch-back ride or, worse still, a single sudden dip in an otherwise flat stretch of road. When you are approaching the top of a rise, you cannot see into the next dip.*

markings which you will have to drive to the left of, etc. Never 'follow through'; that is – don't follow another vehicle which is overtaking unless you can be sure of completing your overtake safely. The driver you are following will only have judged **his** manoeuvre and will not have considered your needs – that is **your** job. Again, try to assess that you can get well past the other vehicle and get his front in your rear view mirror before moving back to the left. (This allows him to maintain his safety gap behind you.) If there is a need to get back in earlier than that, you probably should not have started to overtake in the first place.

Inevitably mistakes are made. Should you ever find yourself in a position where you need to move back to the left earlier than would be ideal, you should consider that it would be better slightly to inconvenience the vehicle you have overtaken than to collide with any oncoming vehicle. In this circumstance you must make sure you do not strike or force off the road the vehicle you have just overtaken.

Usually road markings (ranging from a hazard warning centre line to a double white middle line) show you where it would be inappropriate to cross the centre line in order to overtake. Take special care on this type of road section; you will be surprised at how many other drivers think they know better than the road markings.

Also to be considered when overtaking are slip-stream and crosswinds. When you pass another vehicle, the effect of either can cause buffeting to both you and him. A firmer hold on your steering may be needed as you emerge into a crosswind from which you have been shielded by the other vehicle.

The Highway Code reminds you of the clearance you should allow when passing horses, cyclists and motorcyclists. You must watch out for motorcyclists suddenly trying to avoid surface hazards. Cats' eyes, tram rails, tar infilling of road cracks – especially when wet – all threaten their balance and can precipitate skids.

The Code defines only one circumstance when you are allowed to overtake on the left: when the vehicle in front is signalling to turn right and you have room to pass on the left safely.

However, it does acknowledge that an exception must be made when traffic is moving *slowly* in queues. When members of the queue to your right are moving slower than those in your queue you may pass by on their left. (This means in stop/start/creep moving, not in 70 mph ''queues'' or in *normal flowing* traffic on dual carriageways.) Other rules warn you not to change lanes to the left or to weave in and out so as to overtake.

This rule does not mention one-way streets. The conditions for passing on the left here should depend on an element of either situation (above) existing as well. However, traffic may pass either side of you. Indeed, you can sometimes be passed on both sides at once!

You are advised against swapping lanes in an effort to get to the front of queues of traffic. It is a dangerous practice because it increases the risk of collision, particularly with two-wheelers (who can nip between the queues) and pedestrians, who try to take advantage of the slow-moving traffic in order to cross. As I mentioned earlier, it rarely gains you more than a few seconds, and from a safety point of view it annoys some motorists so much that they become incensed and drive aggressively until they have 'got you back' or your journeys take different directions. This might not be for some time.

Some drivers think it is either clever or funny to speed up when they are being overtaken. This is a very dangerous practice. It means the vehicle which is overtaking will not be able to complete the manoeuvre as the driver had planned. If this results in his being unable to get back into the left lane before he meets another vehicle head-on, or before he reaches an island or road marking which he must keep to the left of, the driver who is keeping him out there is responsible for whatever results. I have seen drivers speed up to 'hold off' another vehicle and, when the overtaking driver realised what was happening and tried to drop back, slow down at the same rate to keep him in peril for longer. Why is there never a policeman there when this happens?

If another driver is determined to overtake your vehicle, remember it is not your job to try and make him stick to speed limits etc. Whatever he may do – flashing headlights, driving too close – do not let him intimidate you into exceeding the speed limit. Ensure that you drive correctly and on a predictable course so that he can find his safest opportunity to get past. This might even entail you slowing down a little, to increase the gap in front of your car, in order for him to get back to the left after he has overtaken you. If he cuts in on you, do not retaliate. Give him the benefit of the doubt – he might be a doctor on an emergency call without his flashing green light.

If your side of the road is blocked by an obstruction such as a parked vehicle or road works, you should give way to vehicles approaching from the opposite direction before pulling out to pass the obstruction. If you can see from a distance that there is insufficient room to pass other traffic beside an obstruction, try to meet the traffic in a wider section of the road. Often this only means slowing down until the oncoming vehicles have cleared the narrow section. If you do have to stop, you will probably only have to wait for a short time, so be patient. Try not to stop too close to the obstruction. The further back you can stop, the better your vision round it will be and the more smoothly you will be able to get away afterwards. If you pull up too close you will have to struggle round when it's your turn to go, and this will result in having to pull out further into the wrong side of the road.

When there are obstructions on both sides of the road, try to be courteous where possible and particularly on hills. If, for instance, you are coming down hill, give way to another vehicle which is coming up. After all, it is much easier for you to get restarted than it would be for him.

In one rule the Highway Code names five places where you **MUST NOT** overtake. In the couple of rules following comes a substantial list of places where you are warned **DO NOT** overtake. For me these places rank just as highly and sometimes more so. The only difference seems to be that these may never have been named specifically in any particular Act of law.

Always remember: **if in doubt – do not overtake.**

Another time not to overtake is when you are following a vehicle with its indicator on but its driver seems not to be aware of it. He may or he *may not* have simply forgotten to cancel it after a previous use.

8

JUNCTIONS

Before dealing with junctions, I want to define something which I will mention a few times in the next section, 'the flow'.

The 'flow' is a concept, rather than an object or situation. It is a safe speed, which varies between zero and the speed limit for the road you are using. It is a speed at which you feel you are making satisfactory progress for the road, weather and traffic conditions, without holding up other traffic, and at which you would feel comfortable for your chauffeur to drive you about in your Rolls-Royce. When you achieve the 'flow', you will consistently be in the correct road position, driving at the correct speed for the situation, in the correct gear for that speed. Both major and minor adjustments to these factors will run together fluently, smoothly, accurately reflecting and anticipating the ever-changing circumstances ahead. You will feel that you have complete control of your vehicle and have plenty of time to deal safely with whatever may happen next. You will know when you achieve 'the flow' because it will **feel** right.

I would also like to point out here, that many accidents happen at junctions – most of them caused by people (not always drivers) not looking properly, or drivers not taking enough care about the control of their vehicles. Bad observation, positioning, and/or approaching junctions too fast results in incorrect and often dangerous routes being taken. Those factors also mean that should someone or something move into your path, you will have difficulty stopping in time or avoiding them. I do not want to horrify you with lists of things which are done incorrectly or things which bad drivers do, but you must accept that junctions have to be treated with due regard for their in-built dangers.

The Highway Code rules on road junctions remind you to take extra care as junctions are particularly dangerous for cyclists, motorcyclists and pedestrians. The best way to be certain that you are not going to endanger them, yourself or other drivers at junctions is to have an all-inclusive, well-practised, basic routine. One which will make sure you have taken every possible aspect into consideration. If your routine confirms it is safe to complete your manoeuvre at the junction, then do it. If not, don't.

I adjust my basic routine for different types of junctions. I will deal first with the four main types of turn.

1.   Turning left from a major road into a minor road.
2.   Turning right from a major road into a minor road.
3.   Turning left from a minor road into a major road.
4.   Turning right from a minor road into a major road.

Within these categories naturally come various sub-divisions, such as turns on dual carriageways, at roundabouts and mini-roundabouts, with or without traffic lights, with or without filter lights and so on. Then there are complications like bus and cycle lanes to consider too.

First, you must be able to determine which is a major road and which is a minor one.

Usually, a minor road joins into a major road from the side. Usually, though not always, it will have either Give-Way lines (two broken white lines – sign 117, page 128) or a Stop line (a broad, solid white line – sign 120) across where it meets the major road, and these are normally accompanied by Give-Way or Stop sign(s) respectively (signs 28, 50, 51, 52 from pages 100 and 105). All of these indicate the point where traffic, wanting to join the major road, would have to give way or stop. In some places, such as on residential estates, give-way markings and signs are not used. In these situations, it is necessary for you the road user to be able to tell the difference, and to know which road has priority. (See also *Unmarked Crossroads* page 65.)

The following examples are on junctions *without* traffic light control. Where traffic lights are present, they will determine which stream of traffic has priority.

Example 1. The routine for a left turn, major road to minor road
a) Having ascertained where the road you want to turn into is located, check your interior rear view mirror, to see where any following vehicle is.

Then check your left door mirror, to make sure you do not have a two-wheeler (motorised or pedal-powered) on your left. If one is following you or if you have recently overtaken one, it may catch

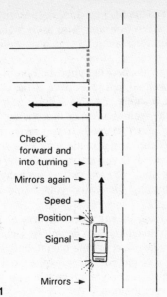

Check
forward and
into turning →

Mirrors again →

Speed →

Position →

Signal →

Mirrors →

Example 1

you up as you slow for the corner.

b) Then signal left. The timing of your signal must make it clear where you are intending to turn. Be careful, if there are two turnings close together, that other road users or pedestrians do not think you are signalling for one turning when in fact you will be taking the other. Too early a signal could also be misinterpreted as a signal for pulling up before the turning. Too late a signal would not give enough warning to anyone who needs to see it, and could result in another road user making a decision which would be dangerous, e.g. a pedestrian stepping off the kerb.

Warning! Remember: your signal (as with any signal) gives notice of your intention but *does not give you any right* to proceed with your manoeuvre unless it is safe.

c) Next, make sure your vehicle is in the correct road position for turning left. You should be towards the left of your half of the road, but no closer than one metre from the kerb, or one metre from any parked vehicles. If you get any closer to the kerb, it will make your driving line through the corner so tight as to make it difficult to remain in your own half of the road after you have turned the corner. Once you have put your vehicle into the correct position for the turn, it should not be necessary to swing out towards the right before turning left. Drivers who do this endanger others who may have already started to overtake them as they slow for the corner. Keep a look out for large vehicles which sometimes need to take a wider path.

At the same time as checking your road position, you should be adjusting your speed so that you arrive at the corner at a suitable speed to negotiate it safely, and in a suitable gear (normally second gear) to drive away from the corner in a smooth manner until you achieve the 'flow' for that road. If you arrive too fast, you will again make it difficult to get round without swinging over to the wrong side of the road. If you arrive too slowly, or slow down too early, others may think you are pulling up before the turn, rather than taking the turning. Basically, you should be able to 'flow' round the corner.

Never coast (clutch down) round corners as this reduces your overall control particularly on downhill sections and corners. Coasting removes the effect of your engine-braking helping to keep your speed down (which it does whilst your foot is off the accelerator) and also means you are not in gear when you want to accelerate away from the turn.

Remember, it is your brake-lights which indicate to any following vehicles that you are slowing down. If the vehicle in your rear view mirror is close enough to need a signal, don't just ease off the gas to let your vehicle slow down. Use your brakes.

d) Having done all the above steps, check your mirrors again (and – with a glance across your shoulder – your blind spot). This time to see where the following vehicle is now that you have slowed down a bit, and to check if any idiot has tried to squeeze up on your near-side despite your signal. This does happen – especially if you have had to wait for any reason.

e) Before actually turning, check into the road where you are heading. Look for pedestrians about to cross the turning. Remember, they have priority if they step into the roadway. Also, look for parked vehicles which you will have to avoid when you pick your steering route away from the turn.

f) If you consider it is safe to proceed with the turn, follow the kerb round the corner and drive away smoothly in the correct road position. Try to achieve the 'flow' as soon as possible.

Example 2. The right turn from a major road into a minor road
This is a very similar routine to the equivalent left turn, except for some obvious differences.

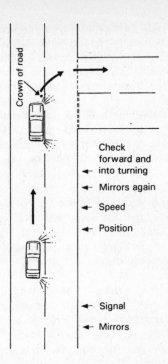

Example 2

a) First, identify your turning. Then, at a suitable distance, check your rear view and driver's door mirrors. Like the left turn, you need to know if there is a vehicle behind yours, and if there is, how far back. You also need to know if anyone is in an overtaking position.

b) Assuming you are not being, or about to be, overtaken at this time, signal right and, if it is safe, move into the turning right position. This is just to the left of the centre of the road. If there is a centre line, stay just to the left of it. If not, you will have to use your judgment to decide where the centre of the road is.

c) Next, adjust your speed. If it is possible to drive round without having to wait, most such turnings can be taken in second gear. Therefore, you have got to get your speed down (using your brakes) and select second gear.

At this stage, you should check your mirrors again. It is not unknown for other motorists to try to overtake at this stage, even when you have followed the procedure to the letter.

d) Next, you must check for traffic coming from the opposite direction. They would have priority over you if they were coming straight past you, or turning into the same road. If there is any such traffic, you should assess whether you will be able to cross its path, into the turning, safely. You now make 1 of 2 choices. (Notice that choice 1 also applies if there is no oncoming traffic.)

Choice 1. If you decide it is safe, check into the turning for pedestrians crossing, and for parked vehicles which will need to be avoided. If you have confirmed it is safe – proceed with your turn from the crown of the road*. Be careful not to swing left before you turn right.

Choice 2. If you decide it is not safe because of oncoming traffic, pedestrians crossing or some other hold-up into the turning – wait about one-and-a-half metres before the crown of the road until it is safe, then check in all directions again (including mirrors and – directly – your blind spot) and proceed with your turn.

The correct waiting position, in which the car is shown in my diagram, is also the best place to start your turn from, as to go past it necessitates oversteering (swan-necking) to get back to your route round the corner. Turning before it usually means cutting the corner and could result in meeting other vehicles head-on as they approach the junction.

Though you have priority over anyone turning right from the minor road, remember that mistakes can be made. Be aware that some drivers may try to turn out in front of you, either because they have not looked properly, or because they think they can race out of your way without affecting your turn.

When you have negotiated your turn, get into your correct road position and achieve the 'flow' as soon as possible.

Remember, when a vehicle you are travelling behind signals left or right, it is either intending to turn or pull over. Both will necessitate slowing down, so always be prepared to slow down yourself.

T-Junctions

A turning from a minor road into a major road (other than at a crossroads) is often described as a T-Junction. Unless the road you

---

* What is commonly referred to as the crown of the road is the point where the centre of the road you are turning into would cross the centre line of the major road.

are turning into is a one-way street, or some other directional limitation is present, you can obviously turn both to the right or the left. There are three basic types of T-Junction:

a) **Closed:** Where you cannot see along the road you are about to join until you are at the Give-Way/Stop line (buildings or fences etc. are blocking your view). This type of situation means you will have to make your decision about the safety of proceeding into the major road **at** the Give-Way or Stop line.

b) **Open:** Where nothing is blocking your view of the road you are about to join (open fields etc., either side of your minor road). It is sometimes possible to make your decision about proceeding into the major road early and this might allow you to 'flow' better.

c) **Obstructed:** Where not only is your view restricted on approach by buildings etc., but in addition by vehicles parked in the major road. When this situation occurs, it is always necessary to stop at the line first. From there you may be able to get a clear view behind the parked vehicles. If however, a parked vehicle is large, or there is more than one, you may still not be able to get a clear view from the line. You then need to 'creep and peep'.

Creeping and peeping necessitates you having to imagine there is a second Give-Way line, level with the far side of the parked vehicles. Using the assumption that other vehicles passing them will be allowing a one metre clearance, you should be able to creep out in first gear, with care, to the imaginary line without causing them to take evasive action. You will have a much better view of the traffic on the major road from here. Keep a special look out for cyclists when creeping out, as they sometimes do not stay one metre out, but swing back in when there are large gaps (such as across junctions) between parked vehicles.

Example 3. Turning left from a minor road into a major road
As I have mentioned before, there are usually five hazard lines included in the approach to a Give-Way or Stop line. These will help you to gauge your speed of approach to the junction correctly.

At a suitable distance from the corner, check your rear view and left door mirrors. If you are satisfied that it is safe, signal left.

Adopt the correct road position (one metre from the kerb etc.) and start to adjust your speed. For closed and obstructed junctions, you will probably have to stop even if you are approaching a Give-Way sign (as opposed to a Stop sign, where you **MUST** stop)

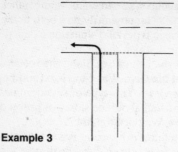

Example 3

so bring your speed down smoothly; arrive at the line gently†.

If you can select first gear just before you stop, this will enable you to move off as soon as you have a safe opportunity to do so, but remember, a Give-Way line means you **MUST** give way to traffic on the major road **and** pedestrians wanting to cross.

Depending on which type of junction it is, when you are in a suitable position to see properly, decide if you can go on safely, or not. You should primarily be looking for vehicles coming from your right, with special care being taken regarding pedestrians wishing to cross in front of you, and cyclists/motorcyclists who are often harder to see than cars, etc. You should not ignore traffic coming from your left, because they may have to drive wide in the road to get past obstructions and could therefore be using the part of the road you will be turning into. It is also worth checking to the left, just before you move off, to see if any vehicles are parked, or may have pulled up in order to drop passengers, since you last checked your path away from the corner.

I always suggest you look both ways a minimum of twice, before you make your decision to proceed. Remember, it is movement you notice. With two looks, your senses register the changes from look one to look two.

If there is traffic using the major road, which necessitates you having to make a decision about the safety of moving off into a gap between vehicles, you should apply the following: *Never pull out, if doing so would make other vehicles have to slow down, stop or move over.*

If – having looked across your shoulder to be certain no one has been hidden in your blind spot – you decide it is safe to go, check

---

† *Remember how alarming it is when you see a vehicle arriving at a junction to your left too fast. It makes you think they are coming straight out without stopping.*

finally to the right again once you are sure you are lined up correctly for your turn, then move off smoothly and try to achieve the correct road position and the 'flow' as soon as possible – unless that final check reveals that you must still wait.

Example 4. Right turn from a minor road into a major road

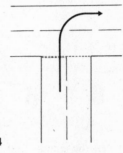

Example 4

Very similar to the left turn, except that you will be signalling right and positioning just to the left of the centre of the road. You usually have to stop at the line when turning right because you will have to ascertain whether there is a safe gap through the traffic coming from your right, allowing you access to another safe gap in the traffic coming from your left. The same rule should be applied – *do not make other vehicles slow down, stop, or move over* in order for you to complete your manoeuvre. Of course, if the major road runs one-way from your left, you must remember to change your routine and look that way first.

Remember your blind spot and to take special care because of pedestrians and cyclists. When you make your decision to go you are going to act on it straightaway, so make sure your decision is correct. You should endeavour to move directly to the correct road position in the major road. Do not pull out and wait at the centre line of the major road (half-way) unless there is a safe refuge, such as in a dual carriageway, which allows you to wait without either end of your vehicle obstructing the path of passing traffic.

Never pull out and travel down the centre line hoping you can move to the correct road position later. This is a very dangerous (though commonly used) practice. It creates an extra lane of traffic in a position where there should be none. Imagine what would happen if another vehicle was doing the same thing in the opposite direction . . .

Having attained the correct road position, get the 'flow' as soon as possible.

Example 5. Exit right from a one-way

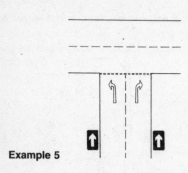

Example 5

Remember also, that when the minor road from which you are turning right is a one-way street (as above), the correct position before your turn is on the right-hand side of the road. If you fail to position correctly, not only will it make your own turn more difficult, but it could also delay other vehicles turning left from the same road. Your blind spot needs checking too – as always.

Priorities at crossroads

Crossroads (fig 8) differ from T-junctions in that you must also have it clear in your head who has priority in the various combina-

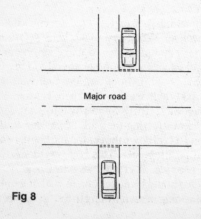

Major road

Fig 8

tions which could exist between you and the traffic approaching from the opposite direction.

In **all** of the following situations, you must acknowledge first and foremost that **you both have to give way to vehicles using the major road**. They definitely have priority over you both.

On top of that you must each take account of the correct priorities as between yourselves. *Examples 3 and 4*, pages 59 and 61, have highlighted already all other considerations you need to make. Those apply equally to a crossroads as they do to T-junctions.

If you are both going straight ahead (fig 9) you have equal priority with each other and should both be able to move across the major road, using the first safe gap in the major road traffic.

Fig 9

If either of you is going straight ahead while the other is turning left (fig 10) your priorities do not affect each other.

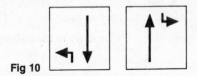

Fig 10

If you are both turning left (fig 11) again your priorities will not affect each other and you can each take your respective first safe opportunity to move off.

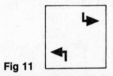

Fig 11

If you are turning left, with him turning right (fig 12) you have priority over him. This is because you are only joining in with the traffic flow, whilst he will have to cross the path of traffic in order to complete his turn. This priority applies even if he was waiting at the junction before you arrived. Beware, some misguided drivers think 'first come first served', but that principle is **wrong**.

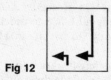

Fig 12

Conversely, if you are turning right and he is turning left (fig 13) he has priority over you for the same reasons.

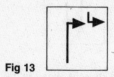

Fig 13

If you are going straight ahead whilst he is turning right (fig 14) you have priority over him, because he would otherwise have to cross your path to complete his turn.

Fig 14

Likewise, if you are turning right, with him coming straight ahead (fig 15) he has priority over you, for the same reason.

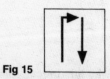

Fig 15

If you are both turning right (fig 16) you should normally pass each other off-side (driver's side) to off-side.

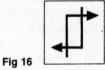

Fig 16

However, if the road is marked with arrows to show that you should pass near-side to near-side, that is the way you should go. Be aware that this presents difficulty in seeing other traffic which is coming straight ahead from the opposite direction. Watch carefully for oncoming traffic, especially motorcycles – so much more easily hidden – to which you must give way. Also be aware that some drivers try to pass near-side to near-side when these markings are *not* present.

Sometimes, when you are both turning right, one or other of you might decide that to struggle round behind the other turning vehicle would be too much of an effort or that lack of space will lead to gridlock if you do attempt it. In this event it is not unusual for whoever decides first to hold back and yield priority to the other. A strictly unofficial nod of the head given direct to the other driver if you are going to wait may help; this is less likely to be misinterpreted than a wave of the hand or flash of headlights. If the other vehicle gives you the priority, do not go without first ensuring it is safe to do so. **Remember**, even when following these guidelines on priority you can **never take it for granted**. You only ever **have** priority **when others give it to you**.

Unmarked Crossroads
Sometimes you will encounter an unmarked crossroads. You must be aware that **no-one** has priority at these. Do not assume, for example, that because one road may be wider that that gives it any extra priority. Traffic from all directions must approach with extreme care and be prepared to stop if necessary. The same applies when traffic lights are not working.

Controlled Junctions
When any junction is controlled by traffic lights you **MUST** obey them. Make sure you are in the correct lane for your required

destination. Make sure you know which lights are controlling your lane. Remember, a green light only means go **if it is safe to do so**.

You must also take account of any signs or arrows on the road applying to your stream of traffic. Some may tell you what you must do like 'straight ahead only' (sign 3), whilst some may indicate what you must not, like 'no left turn' (sign 11).

Also keep a look out for bus and cycle lanes having a different stopping position (often further forward) at some controlled junctions. Remember to allow them to get away safely without hindrance.

Roundabouts (including mini-roundabouts)

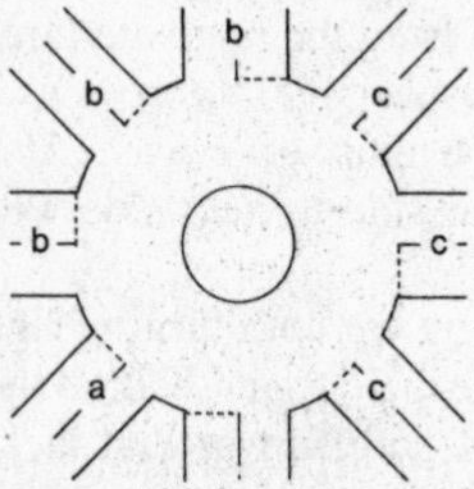

Fig 17

The Highway Code rules are pretty comprehensive, but I have a little to add to them. There can be roads going off in every direction, as in fig 17.

Planning your route through a roundabout starts when you see the sign which shows the possible destinations you can reach from it. This sign usually (though not always 100% accurately) shows the layout of the roundabout. You can tell for instance whether your road is (a) the first turning left, (b) any other turning between the first left and straight ahead (12 o'clock on a clock face), and (c) any turning after 12 o'clock.

I simplify the positioning and signalling routines in such a way that it is standardised for roundabouts which have any number of exits above three. Whichever route you intend to take, you should arrive at the roundabout at a speed and in the appropriate gear (nearly always second) which would allow you to proceed smoothly if it is safe, or stop gently if necessary. Beware, some large vehicles may have to adapt their route in order to complete their passage through roundabouts. Be prepared to hang back rather than risk getting tangled up with them.

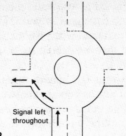

Fig 18

a) If you are turning left as in fig 18 (that is the **first** exit from the roundabout), approach in the left lane, signalling left. Give way to traffic on the roundabout (coming from your right). Remember, you should not make them slow down, stop, or move over. Use the left lane of the roundabout and exit (still signalling left).

b) If you are going straight ahead as in fig 19 (that is – any turning after the first, up to and including the 12 o'clock turning) approach in the left lane, but do not signal. (You may use an outer lane of two or the middle lane of three if the left-hand lane is blocked.) Give way to traffic on the roundabout (coming from your right). If you have started in the left-hand approach lane (which I recommend for beginners) use the left lane of the roundabout. Signal left as you **pass** the exit before the one you want. Exit using the left lane if possible.

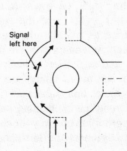

Fig 19

If you approached in the right-hand lane of two or a centre lane of three, take care to go round *in this lane* (even if lanes are not marked specifically all round). When you prepare to exit remember that anyone who *has* used the left lane all round may be vulnerable

– you must not cut them off as you enter the exit road. Equally, in theory, they ought not to cut ahead of you. Thus all parties need to take care. Ideally your exit road will have the same number of lanes as your entry road and the roundabout itself, and you can keep in the same lane throughout.

Beware! A driver to your left may decide to swing on round in front of you to the right just as you are about to exit straight on. He would almost certainly be in the wrong (as he must give way to his right) but it's a pity to allow this all-too-common error to lead to any accident. Be prepared.

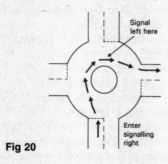

Fig 20

c) Any turning after 12 o'clock (fig 20) counts as a right turn and you can encounter much the same problems when you come to that exit too. Approach in the right-hand lane (or towards the right if only one lane), signalling right. Give way to traffic on the roundabout (coming from your right). Use the right-hand lane of the roundabout and continue to signal right until you **pass** the exit before the one you want. As you pass this exit, check your interior and near-side mirrors and signal left. Check your near-side blind spot to make sure you can move safely into the left lane without cutting across other vehicles and, subsequently, turn left into your exit. Where your exit road has more than one lane available you may select the most appropriate one to your speed and in relation to any other traffic. For beginners the left-hand lane is the natural choice.

Some roundabouts – especially mini-roundabouts – have only three exits (see figs 21A and 21B). Signal when you pass the place where a normal roundabout could be expected to have a turning in order to give other traffic a clear message of your intention to take the next exit. Follow exactly the same rules, incidentally, at

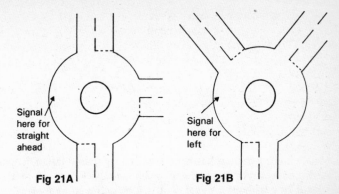

Signal here for straight ahead

Fig 21A

Signal here for left

Fig 21B

mini-roundabouts, as at any other. Note that cars are expected to go round (not over) the white centre circle (even though large lorries may have no alternative but to ride partly across it) and keep a very close eye on how the cramped space is likely to affect what anyone else sharing the roundabout may do. U-turners and right turners who omit to signal are a particular danger.

If there are more than two lanes on the approach to a roundabout, I suggest you still stick to the methods I have recommended above unless the lanes are specifically marked for use with the left, straight or right exits. It's best to avoid the centre lane of three until you have gained quite a lot of experience. This is simply because it is usually the centre lane which gets squeezed if any lane does.

Discounting at Roundabouts

This is my expression for being able to tell (at a glance) which vehicles I must give way to at roundabouts. It may seem a little long-winded at first, but after a little practice you will be surprised how quickly you will be able to make the correct decision every time. This in turn will make roundabouts simpler and safer to use.

Look at the diagram (fig 22) and imagine you are entering the roundabout from entrance A. Depending on where you wish to exit from the roundabout, you will be able to discount vehicles coming from certain directions, provided you can accurately interpret their required exits.

For instance, let us assume you are going to turn left (leave by exit B).

Left-hand lane traffic

You can **discount** any vehicles entering by entrances B, C, or D if

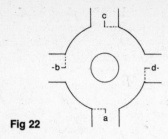

Fig 22

they are entering in their left-hand lane and signalling left. You can also discount any vehicle entering by entrance B or C in the left-hand lane without a signal as it will be going straight ahead.

Any vehicle entering from entrance D in the left-hand lane without a signal is going to exit B and you will have to **give way** to it.

Right-hand lane traffic
Vehicles entering from entrance B in the right-hand lane and signalling right are either going to leave by exit A, or going completely round the roundabout to leave by exit B. You should be able to tell which by the time such a vehicle is passing exit D, as this is where it should start signalling left if it is leaving at exit A.

The question here is: can I get into the flow without making him slow down, stop, or move over even if he does turn out to be going back whence he came?

A vehicle entering from entrance C in the right-hand lane and signalling right is either going to leave by exit B, or going completely round the roundabout. Again, you should be able to tell which by the time it is passing exit A.

Vehicles entering from entrance D in the right-hand lane and signalling right are either going to leave by exit C, or going completely round. Your decision here is basically the same: can I get into the flow, etc? Normally the answer will be yes, but is dependent on the width of road around the roundabout and on how well he stays in the right lane of it and you in the left.

You can adapt this discounting idea as you approach each roundabout and, provided you have picked up the layout from the signs, it should enable you to make your journey through the roundabout easier. You will be able to discount vehicles which cannot affect your route, and concentrate on those which you need to consider more thoroughly.

Always make sure, once you have decided to go, that none of the discounted vehicle drivers have changed their minds and altered their course so as to interfere with your route. Remember, large vehicles may have to take extra room, or different lanes entirely, to achieve their required route.

Don't forget that horse riders and sometimes cyclists will use the left-hand lane to reach whichever exit they want, so look out for them riding straight past exits. Hold well back as necessary.

There are another couple of items worth considering at this stage. Firstly, unless they are provided with proper crossings at roundabouts, pedestrians have to cross the roads where and when they can. Quite often they will be attempting to cross while your attention is elsewhere, so remember to keep a look out for them.

Secondly, remember that the driver in front of you may not move forward onto the roundabout when **you** think it is safe for him so to do. Learners, the inexperienced, and the otherwise preoccupied will sometimes let a suitable opportunity go without taking advantage of it. Make sure your road ahead is clear before you proceed, thus avoiding becoming another episode the like of which starts "I was waiting for a gap in the traffic at this roundabout, minding my own business, when this idiot shunts me right up the . . ."

Finally, remember that some drivers do not always signal correctly and others sometimes make mistakes. *Never trust a signal until the speed and positioning of the vehicle confirms it.*

Reversing

In your Practical Driving Test you will have to be able to (a) reverse round a corner (to the left or the right – the latter usually only if you take your Test in a van); (b) reverse (parallel) park; and (c) turn your vehicle in the road to face the opposite direction, using forward and reverse gears. Your examiner will only ask you to demonstrate your skill in two out of the three exercises, but as it will be his choice you must be adept at them all.

If you make an error in your positioning when reversing during your driving test, do not throw your hands up thinking you will have failed. Provided you realise the error has occurred, the ability to safely rectify the mistake may save the day. The trick in all reversing exercises is to observe all around often enough to ensure safety, and to keep your car slow and in control in order to make it do what you set out to achieve in the manoeuvre.

Before all of these manoeuvres you must ask yourself a set of questions.

1. Is it safe? You are responsible for the safety of pedestrians and other road users. Never attempt any manoeuvre on or near a pedestrian crossing, where there are children playing in the street, or too near a corner – except for (a) – or a busy entranceway.

2. Is it convenient? Do not contemplate a manoeuvre if it would badly disrupt the normal flow of traffic, or if parked vehicles would make your manoeuvre particularly difficult to execute.

3. Is it legal (and/or in accordance with the Highway Code)? For (a) never reverse from a minor road into a major road. Never reverse into a one-way street because you will pass a No-Entry sign or a One-Way sign in the wrong direction, either on the way in or on the way out. For (b) there are so many places where you cannot legally park that I am not going to list them here; however, clearly you must not attempt (b) at any such place. For (c) you **MUST NOT** turn your car round on motorways, dual carriageways, in one-way streets or anywhere there is a No U-turn sign.

4. How do I control the car throughout the manoeuvre? You have to consider:
    * the use of clutch control and/or brakes in order to make the car move slowly;
    * whether the terrain is flat, up hill or down hill, or a combination of the three;
    * the amount of steering you will require, and so on.

For (a) the mechanical skill of how much and when to steer you will get from the person teaching you and from experience (practice). You will need to know how to pull in safely before beginning the manoeuvre. You will be required to stay about half to one metre from the kerb throughout. You will have to demonstrate to your examiner that you can keep control, observe adequately, mainly using your back window but never forgetting that you need to know what is happening all around, and safely negotiate the corner backwards to end up parallel with the kerb, far enough back from the corner to be able to adopt the correct position at the junction for turning right. (The examiner will tell you when to stop reversing.) Remember, as you steer to turn the back end of the car in, the front will swing out. This could affect other vehicles using the same section of road, so make sure you keep a look out both ways for them and be prepared to stop and wait if it looks like you might impede their journey past.

For (b) you will be asked to stop alongside a car which is parked beside a kerb. You will have to be able to demonstrate that you can park behind that vehicle in a gap which is the size of two cars. There will not be another vehicle at the other end of the gap – you will have to judge the length yourself. You will be expected to end up close to the kerb, with your wheels straight and your vehicle parallel to the kerb. Though it is obviously best to be able to get into that position in one movement, it is still acceptable if you need to take an extra shunt to straighten up. Do not touch the kerb. Remember, many roads slope down towards the gutter. This means the weight of your car will possibly try to rush the last bit for you.

For (c) commonly referred to as 'a three-point-turn', the examiner will normally find a section of road where it is possible to turn in three 'strokes'; but it is permitted, if you need it, to take five or even more if the circumstances demand it. You will be required to demonstrate that you are controlling the car properly, observing properly (all round) and completing the manoeuvre safely without too much waste of time or holding up of other road users. Remember, most roads slope down towards the pavements and up towards the centre line, so this must be considered when working out your clutch/gas/brake control.

You must accept that, whenever you are reversing, you must give way to everyone. That is: other vehicles, pedestrians, cycles and so on. If you cannot see behind your vehicle, you are expected to seek help to see you back. Keep a special look out for blind pedestrians. They may hear your engine moving the car, but cannot always determine which direction you are travelling. Consider that a pedestrian might be deaf, too. Also keep a special look out for prams, pushchairs and wheelchair users. Remember they are unable to travel sideways and cannot always get out of your way. It is your responsibility to make sure you do not endanger these other road users. One last thing – it is illegal to reverse further than necessary. Drivers who reverse a couple of hundred metres rather than turn round and go back are not only dangerous, but risking prosecution.

9

LIGHTS AND HORNS

The Highway Code reflects the law regarding the use and maintenance of your vehicle lighting. The rules tell you when you must
use the different lights available: sidelights, dim-dip, dipped or
main-beam headlights and fog lights.

When and how to use your lights
One of my instructions to pupils is 'never be afraid to be the first
vehicle with your lights on'. You will notice certain vehicles, such
as Volvos, with their sidelights on all the time. This is because they
are manufactured in Sweden where the law requires all vehicles to
have daylight running lights. When it starts to get dark or gloomy
because of impending rain and so on, you will notice that vehicles
with their lights on are easier to see. By putting my dim-dips on I
make my car easier for other drivers to notice. It prompts other
drivers to switch their lights on too.

Note that in daytime fog or when you cannot see more than 100
metres, you **MUST** have headlights and rear sidelights on. In fog at
night headlights and rear sidelights are likewise compulsory. Note:
plain headlights are advised for dull days too.

You may *choose*, also, to use front and/or rear fog lights during
daylight or darkness –
1. ONLY in addition to headlights and rear sidelights NEVER as
    a substitute and
2. ONLY whilst visibility is seriously reduced – defined as being
    down to 100 metres or less.

In such extreme conditions, my advice is DO use them but
remember – ALL specifically fog-only lights **MUST** be switched
off directly visibility improves.

Even in normal daylight conditions, rain-drops on the windows
will reduce the clarity of all round vision. I therefore make it a rule
– if I have to switch on my wipers – that I also switch on my lights
to make my vehicle more visible.

On some modern vehicles sidelights and dim-dip operate from the same switch position. Sidelights show when the ignition is switched off, but once the engine is running they upgrade to dim-dip. These are sufficient to drive in town after dark provided the street lighting is bright enough to illuminate your way. If this is not the case, you must use your dipped headlights. Obviously, if your car does not have dim-dip you must use dipped headlights anyway.

Dazzle
At night, immediately you leave a lit-up area, you should use main-beam headlights whenever the road ahead is clear of traffic. However, you should be careful in the use of main-beams to ensure you do not dazzle other road users. You should switch to dipped-beam when there is a vehicle approaching (even a bicycle) from the opposite direction, when there is a vehicle travelling in front of yours, when you enter a lit-up area and in fog. In fog main-beams glare back at you; dipped-beams allow you to see the road surface better. (The same applies in daytime fog.)

Remember at night that when you reduce from main to dipped beam you will reduce the distance that you can effectively see; therefore you must also consider a speed reduction in order still to be able to stop within the distance you know is clear.

If you are dazzled by an oncoming vehicle, concentrate your view on your own side of the road and slow down. You should be prepared to stop if necessary. Never be tempted to flash your headlights at it. That could create the situation where you are both dazzled, a good recipe for an accident.

If you are dazzled in your rear view (interior) mirror, use the anti-dazzle flip-up. This will distort the view behind, but still allows you to see that headlights are there. If you have a persistent, glaring follower, consider allowing him to pass but never retaliate.

Equally, **you** should take care when changing to main beam from dipped beam. Using the above example of dazzle from behind – when you are overtaking at night, do not switch to main beam before you are level with the vehicle you are passing. Its driver, of course, should be using main beam if there is nothing coming towards you both. This helps you see ahead whilst you are overtaking. Naturally, he should dip his headlights as you pass him.

Finally – on the subject of switching your lights on – be careful when you do it. Take care not to switch them on whilst there is a situation in front of you where another road user might think you are signalling him with them.

Headlight flashing

Flashing your headlights **only** means 'I am here and I think you have not noticed me'. The sort of situation where their use can save a nasty incident is where you are overtaking and the driver concerned starts to indicate his intention of pulling out into your path. Sounding your horn may not be heard, but a long (two second) show of your headlights ought to alert the other driver to your presence. This is how it should work. It illustrates that a flash of headlights does **not** mean 'come on out mate'. Beware of two problems here: 1), as he didn't see you in the first instance he may not see your flash either: 2), he may see only part of your flash and **wrongly** interpret this to mean permission to pull out.

Sometimes another driver may give away his priority and enable you to go through a gap, or pull out of a side turning/parking space etc., by flashing his lights or gesturing. Do not take his signal alone as an assurance that it is safe to proceed. Check for yourself before you go on. Judge by his subsequent action not by his unofficial (and incorrect) signal.

Use of the Horn

Basically, you **MUST NOT** use the horn in a built-up area between 11.30 pm and 7.00 am. You **MUST NOT** use it whilst your vehicle is stationary except when another vehicle is about to collide with something or someone unless a warning is given. It is not meant to be used to let your friends know that you are waiting outside their house, or for giving noisy vent to anger.

10

TEMPORARY STOPS AND PARKING

The Highway Code states the rules on waiting and parking. It gives general advice about the care which should be taken when parking, etc., and gives a few specific things which should be looked out for. It also states that you **MUST** switch off your engine, fog lights and headlights. When motorists are waiting at the kerb side, they often do not switch their headlights off. This can dazzle other drivers. If it has happened to you, you will know what I mean. Don't do it to others.

The Highway Code continues this section with a list of places where you **MUST NOT** stop or park, and provides examples of places where parking or waiting would either endanger or inconvenience pedestrians and other road users. I would emphasise – do not stop, wait or park anywhere which would make it difficult for a fire engine, ambulance or other emergency vehicle to get past.

Purely in the interest of safety – if you have to park on a steep hill, turn your steering slightly towards (facing down hill) or away from (up hill) the kerb. In the unlikely event that your handbrake fails, this measure will put the weight of the car against the kerb and should stop it running away down the hill. As an extra precaution, you should also leave the car in gear – 1st if facing up hill, reverse if facing down and in 'Park' if driving an automatic.

The Highway Code mentions parking spaces which are reserved for specifically authorised users, such as Orange Badge holders. You **MUST NOT** park in any of these spaces without the necessary authority.

It also says you **MUST NOT** park at night facing against the direction of the traffic flow. This is one of my pet hates. Any vehicle parked facing the traffic flow will be reflecting my headlights back at me (my headlights are adjusted to the left and so are theirs) rather than showing me its rear reflector lenses. This is not only misleading, but can be dangerous as it could affect my judgment in narrow sections.

The Highway Code tells us which vehicles **MUST** have lights on if parked after dark. Note the importance of whether a 30 mph speed limit applies. I have observed that not many drivers of large vehicles take notice of these requirements. Though this does not make general driving particularly dangerous, I often wonder what the result would be if the authorities insisted on compliance, perhaps getting a few of the offending drivers out of bed to correct the omission or even prosecuting them.

Always remember to be considerate when opening your doors whilst stopped or parked. Take a good look round to ensure you will not hit a passing vehicle or cyclist on your offside, or a pedestrian on your nearside.

Highway blockages

In the rules which deal with the restrictions on goods vehicles when loading and unloading, there seem to be a couple of **MUST NOT**s which are frequently ignored here as well, e.g. parking on verges, or in the middle of roads, etc.

The Highway Code states that you **MUST NOT** exceed any temporary speed limit imposed at road works. I have noticed a general reluctance of drivers to observe temporary speed restrictions. They seem to take it as a personal slight that they are not allowed to decide for themselves the correct speed to negotiate the road works. This is particularly noticeable at the end of the restriction. Many drivers start to accelerate as soon as they see the sign showing the end of the speed restriction, rather than wait until they reach it. This often results in a free for all, with the vehicles which **are** staying within the restricted speed being used as leap frogs – by other drivers acting as if it were a Grand Prix start.

You are asked to consider other road users if your vehicle breaks down, and to get your vehicle off the road if possible. Of course, this is not always possible and the Highway Code goes on to recommend ways of making your vehicle conspicuous if it is causing an obstruction.

Hazard lights will show other traffic that you are stationary in a position where they would not normally expect a vehicle to be. A warning triangle, if you carry one, should be placed back along the road to help warn approaching traffic of the obstruction ahead. On normal roads, it should be at least 45 metres back. You have to use some common sense when placing your triangle. You don't want to stick it in the way of traffic, but you do want drivers to notice it. If you are causing the obstruction just after a bend or the top of a hill, think how far back would be the best place to warn approaching drivers. It could well be further than the recommended distance. The Highway Code advises that any such warning device should **not** be placed anywhere on a motorway.

The Highway Code also says that at night and in poor visibility, you should not stand behind your vehicle. This would obviously obscure your rear lights and make it more difficult for approaching drivers to judge the situation. Keep sidelights on but don't leave your headlights on if you have had to stop. They could possibly dazzle a driver approaching from the opposite direction.

If anything falls from your vehicle onto the road you should stop and, only if it is safe to do so, retrieve it. This does **not** apply on motorways; on them you should instead call the police from the next emergency telephone.

Accidents

You should be prepared to slow down, or even stop if necessary, when you see signs of an accident or obstruction ahead. Keep a good look out ahead for flashing lights, blue for the emergency services, amber for breakdown recovery vehicles and hazard warning lights on ordinary vehicles. Avoid loitering at incidents if you can. If you have skills which might be needed, such as first aid, try to stop somewhere safe and offer assistance. However, if you cannot be of assistance, do not add to the obstruction by hanging around. If you can get past and away safely, do it.

Once, I drove past the scene of a tragic airliner crash. There were so many drivers pulled up 'rubber-necking', that traffic could only squeeze past with great difficulty. Later, on the television news, they stated that even the emergency services were considerably delayed in getting to the incident because of the traffic jam.

The Highway Code gives sound advice for situations where you are involved in an incident, or if you stop to give assistance. Your main priority is to ensure that you do not make matters worse than they already are. Many people will stop at an accident to see if they can help, but very few seem to think of getting help (police, fire or ambulance) if it is needed.

Always try to establish if one person has taken charge of the incident; if they have, offer your help if appropriate. If nobody has taken charge, take charge yourself. Give clear unambiguous instructions.

1. Send people to keep the incident scene safe by warning/directing traffic.
2. Send someone to make sure all the vehicles at the scene are showing hazard warning lights, their engines are switched off and nobody is smoking.
3. Send someone to get any necessary help, having made sure they know how to describe the correct location, the number of casualties, the extent of any injuries and the involvement, if any, of dangerous goods.
4. Keep casualties warm and never leave them unattended; move them as little as possible. Do not let them drink anything.
5. Make sure you utilise any relevant skills, e.g. don't send a first-aider away to direct traffic.
6. Ensure that uninjured parties to the accident move well off the road out of harm's way, with children and pets under control. (Animals may be safest kept in the vehicles.)
7. One person should be put to work keeping rubber-necks away from the incident.
8. Retain control of the incident until a suitable person relieves you (fire-chief, police officer).

Remember, at any serious incident, if nobody takes control, confusion reigns. However, if one person becomes the incident organiser, most of the 'headless chickens' stop running around and can be put to some useful purpose.

The Highway Code rule which deals with incidents involving dangerous goods brings in one of the most important details. When informing the emergency services, give as much accurate information about casualties, dangerous loads, vehicles involved etc., as possible. This could make the difference between the correct or incorrect vehicles being sent. The exact location will result in the emergency services arriving sooner, etc. This is one good reason to carry pen and paper in your vehicle always.

We should all be as well-informed as possible about first aid. See page 132.

If you yourself are party to any accident you **MUST STOP** and obey the rules in the Highway Code. More about this is on page 131.

11

MOTORWAY DRIVING

The Highway Code does a serious bit of cross-referencing to other Rule numbers here. It is important that you can use the necessary parts of these other Rules in their correct context when driving on motorways. It would probably be a good idea to re-read them now before you go on to this section.

The Code lists the vehicles and drivers who **MUST NOT** use motorways.

It points out that you will probably be travelling faster on the motorway, just as the other traffic will be. This necessitates thinking quickly, planning further in advance than on other roads and observing further ahead.

You also need to drive smoothly on motorways. Try not to do anything suddenly, especially accelerating, steering/swerving violently, or braking. Any of these will make proper control of your vehicle harder as well as making you difficult for other drivers to plan around.

Ensure that your vehicle is fit for the trip on a motorway. Especially pay attention to: tyres, fuel, oil and water, mirrors, lights, reflectors, windows and washer bottles, etc. Any load you are carrying or towing **MUST** be secured properly. You should also prepare yourself. Plan ahead before you start your journey – know your exit number before you join the motorway. Know where the services are, etc.

The Highway Code has a section which covers joining a motorway. It does not, however, mention that as you join from the slip road, you should be signalling right. Do not just look in your driver's door mirror, check the blind spot over your right shoulder. This does save lives. Also make sure you have changed into a gear which gives you some acceleration – this might be needed in order to match the speed of the stream of traffic you will be merging with. Never forget – you cannot just push your way in. Never force another vehicle to slow down, swerve, or anything worse. More on this subject when you reach sign 80 in Chapter 16, page 114.

On the motorway and driving past a slip road where other traffic is joining, try to be considerate. Keep a special look out for vehicles with foreign number plates. They could be left-hand drive and that makes it more difficult for their drivers to get a clear view of your approach, especially in the case of lorries or coaches.

Make sure you have got used to travelling at the speed of other traffic using the motorway before you attempt to start overtaking etc. You soon get used to travelling at speed. There does not seem to be much difference between travelling with other traffic at 30 mph and at 70 mph, except that the safety distances between vehicles must be greater and everything must be done much more smoothly. However, due to the amount of planning needed to overtake or change lanes at the higher speed, it is advisable to get the feel of that speed before 'going for it'.

The Highway Code offers advice regarding tiredness whilst driving. The advice to stop somewhere safe and take a break and/or some refreshment is just as important whenever you feel fatigued. Do not rely on a loud stereo system to keep you awake, or depend on fresh air from open windows to keep you alert. Most experienced drivers will recommend that you do not drive for longer than a couple of hours at a time without having a break. Plan motorway journeys accordingly. Never be tempted to wait too long before you stop. It could be just after you have passed the last services for 50 miles that you suddenly start to feel tired. In that event leave at the next junction off the motorway and find somewhere safe for a break.

You **MUST NOT** reverse on the motorway, even if you have missed your exit. Most of you will have seen television programmes which show police videos of drivers doing this. I expect most of you cannot imagine yourself doing the same thing, even if it means you would have to drive to the next exit (maybe many miles further on). Nevertheless, I fear it happens every day somewhere on our motorways and sometimes with tragic effects.

The Highway Code also says you must not drive against the flow of traffic. Again, police film of this happening and reports of accidents caused by drivers doing just that are not uncommon. When you see or hear of this, you probably ask yourself 'Why were they going down the wrong carriageway?', 'How did they miss the signs?', etc. I ask myself the same questions. The saddest point to this situation is that if such a mistake results in an accident, it is most likely to involve a head-on collision, with some poor innocent soul, who is probably driving correctly along his lane minding his own business.

The last thing he expects to see (possibly the last thing he ever sees) is a vehicle coming towards him head-on. His brain will be attuned to keeping his vehicle safe in the normal situation, where all vehicles are travelling in the same direction. This will make his decision about what to do next a little slow in arriving, because his first thought, on seeing the vehicle coming head-on, will be 'what the ????'. If both vehicles are travelling at 70 mph, they are getting nearly 70 metres closer together every second. That doesn't give him much time to decide his best course of action.

Motorway overtaking

The Code deals with lane discipline, and refers you to the Rules regarding vehicles which are not allowed in the outside lane when there are three or more lanes on the motorway. Do not ignore this information. It helps you to know who is, or is not, allowed into the outside lane when you are planning to overtake.

You **MUST NOT** overtake by using the hard shoulder. Even if the whole carriageway is blocked by ordinary traffic, perhaps stopped by an accident, the hard shoulder must be left free for the emergency services access.

In theory – with no direct right turns off motorways – there can be no normal circumstance in which overtaking on the left is permissible (see page 50). In practice, when sheer weight of traffic means all lanes become congested, traffic in lanes to the left may, from time to time, find itself able to move ahead faster than traffic in lanes to its right. This is allowed but strictly only for the purpose of keeping up with the other drivers in your lane. Study this Code motorway overtaking rule with great care.

For normal motorway overtaking make sure: (a) that you can complete the manoeuvre safely, (b) that you will not have to exceed the speed limit (or break the law any other way) and, (c) that it is necessary to overtake. Often, if the vehicle in front is being driven only just below the speed limit, overtaking is not worth the effort. Likewise if you are just coming up to an exit. The vehicle you are about to overtake may turn off. If **you** are about to turn off, overtaking might take longer than you expected and make you miss your exit, or cause you to risk cutting back in, across the front of the vehicle you have just overtaken. You won't like it when this happens to you; so don't do it to others.

Having checked your rear and driver's door mirrors and decided it will be safe, indicate right. Allow your indicator to flash **at least** three times before moving out into the next lane. Before you move out, check the blind spot (over your right shoulder); this could save your life. Remember, if *you* have decided that you need to overtake the vehicle in front, then the vehicle behind may also be about to overtake as well. Once you have moved out get on and overtake as smoothly as you can. Do not sit in the other driver's blind spot. When you have passed him, check that you can see all of the front of his vehicle in your rear view mirror. (This ensures you will not erode his two-second safety gap.) Then check your left door mirror (and over your left shoulder) to make sure it is safe and, if it is, signal and move back over to the left lane smoothly. When you have overtaken a vehicle, try to keep with the flow of traffic in that lane. Do not slow down immediately you have completed an overtake unless there is a good reason. Nothing annoys other drivers more, except perhaps having you cut back in too early.

You should take care not to make your vehicle a moving obstruction. I never stay in the overtaking lane if it is clear to my left, even if I am travelling at the maximum speed limit. It is not my job to make other drivers stick to the speed limits, and it could well prove dangerous if I tried. I leave that to the police and motorway camera systems. However, if I think a driver is being particularly dangerous I have no reservations about reporting the details to the police.

The Highway Code gives you details regarding motorway signs which are only switched on as and when necessary. Remember, they are there to help you. Do not ignore them just because you cannot see the situation they are dealing with. I have seen vehicles ignoring 'lane closed' signs, only to find themselves having to push in later, rather than get into the correct lane earlier and keep going with the flow. I have seen vehicles ignore temporary speed limits, only to see them nearly pile into the back of an existing hold-up further up the road. Just incidentally, when the amber lights flash, they flash up and down. When the red lights flash, they flash from side to side. This makes you notice them more. Like traffic lights, the red signs mean you **MUST STOP**; they are more than just advisory.

Experimental variable speed limits have been introduced on some motorways. When the flow of traffic in particular lanes necessitates it, the speed limit is changed to allow better overall flow. The logic is that it is better to keep traffic moving at a slower speed than to allow bunching and stopping to occur. The reduction in stress, and possibly in the number of breakdowns and accidents, will be interesting when analysis is done over a decent period of time. In theory any need to overtake disappears. Signs request drivers not to change lanes at all. Doing so annoys other drivers who are complying with the restrictions, and would probably result in the sensors re-juggling the necessary lane speeds to even out the flow again.

The Highway Code tells you **not** to try to recover anything which falls from your vehicle onto the motorway, but to stop at the **next emergency phone** (rather than using a mobile phone) and tell the police (making sure you are facing the approaching traffic whilst making your call; there may be some erratic goings on if an object is lying on the carriageway). It is very important that you do this as quickly as possible. They will need to know the number of the roadside telephone (or the location of the nearest marker post on the hard shoulder), how far before it the item fell off, and where it came to rest (which lane). They will then arrange (if necessary) for the appropriate lanes to be closed from the previous set of signs, and will send a vehicle to recover the item/object safely.

It is possible for things to fall from vehicles without the driver noticing. If you notice an object (which has fallen from another vehicle) causing a hazard on the carriageway, you should follow the above procedure too.

The Code covers stopping and breakdowns whilst using the motorway. Remember, if you do have to pull up on the hard shoulder, leave your wheels turned a little to the left. This should make sure your vehicle is not shunted back onto the motorway, in the event (God forbid) that another hits it on its way past. You might have noticed that this safety precaution is the practice of emergency vehicle drivers. They also tend to stop a few car lengths behind the other vehicle so that if their vehicle is shunted, it will not hit them whilst they are attending to the stopped vehicle.

Keep well clear of your stopped vehicle. Try to get beyond the hard shoulder if this is possible. Statistics prove that the hard shoulder of a motorway is one of the most lethal places on our roads. So don't just sit and be hit. Finally, remember that in the event of a breakdown on a motorway – even a simple one like a puncture – the Highway Code states that you have to call for help. You should not attempt the repairs yourself.

Incidentally, if you see a vehicle stopped on the hard shoulder and displaying a 'HELP' banner, this indicates a disabled person waiting in need of official assistance. It is not your job to stop and offer help; the occupant might well be alarmed if anyone other than a uniformed police officer or expected rescue service were to stop.

Just a few words about rejoining the motorway after you have been stopped on the hard shoulder need adding here. Passing traffic is moving fast, and you will have to ensure there is a large enough gap in the traffic to allow you to get back into the flow. Never forgetting your signal or that there may be other vehicles stuck on the hard shoulder in front of you, you should use the hard shoulder to build up your speed before merging into the driving lane.

I will be covering motorway exit signs later but I always stress that, at the end of every trunk road, there is always a good reason to slow down (sharp turn, roundabout, etc.). After you have been driving at speed for any length of time, you will have grown accustomed to how it feels. When you slow down, initially it will feel as if you are not moving as fast as your speedometer says you are. Beware, it is not easy negotiating roundabouts at 70 mph (this practice should be reserved for professional stunt men).

12

TWO WHEELS AND FOUR LEGS

The most vulnerable road users are pedestrians, cyclists (and motorcyclists) and horse riders. Having already given some attention to pedestrians, we now move on to the cyclists and horse riders. A whole section of the Highway Code rules is directed specifically at extra care for pedestrains, cyclists, animal handlers and horse riders. I do not propose to expand on them all, but recommend you read and understand them as this will help you deal with these road users when you meet them.

By and large, most horse riders and animal handlers take the Highway Code seriously (except for dogs being allowed out on their own or off the lead). However, some cyclists, and not just young ones, seem to delight in ignoring rules.

If you assume that most cyclists will generally ignore the suggestions in the Code, and in a lot of cases break the laws set down, you stand a fair chance of dealing with them correctly.

My rule – treat all cyclists as if they don't know or care anything about the safety of themselves or others.

By way of an example consider the rule which states cyclists **MUST** use front and rear lights and a red rear reflector at night. The number of cyclists who do not, and therefore risk being involved in accidents, is staggering. During a recent after-dark journey of about two miles through my home town, I overtook fourteen cycles. Only six were equipped with lights whilst eight were not. If only they realised how horrifying it is for a driver to suddenly find them in his path, they would surely not do it. Also to be considered at this point is how other motorists interpreted my actions when I encountered these unlit bikes. One of them, I suddenly saw loom out of the darkness into my headlight beam from behind a parked lorry. I had to take avoiding action which entailed swinging out an extra metre. Imagine what the oncoming drivers thought when I changed course for no reason which was apparent to them. Probably the best way to proceed whenever there is a dark section ahead, particularly at junctions and roundabouts, is to assume there will be an unlit cycle in it. Restrict your speed until such time as your headlights confirm otherwise.

I have seen cyclists with very expensive bikes, all the lycra gear, the proper shoes which clip onto the pedals, safety hat and all, but **no lights**. Perhaps parting with a nominal sum to protect your life is not considered macho.

Having stated my rule, I hereby give my unreserved apologies to those cyclists who **do** stick to the rules and ride considerately and safely.

It is a good idea to watch out for cyclists, motorcyclists and horse riders glancing over their right shoulders. This is often an indication that they need to move over to their right (sometimes without any accompanying signal), or that they are about to signal right. Noticing this precursor gives you a little extra time to take whatever action is necessary.

Another thing to consider and be aware of is unattended animals. In town you should always be on the look out for cats and dogs on the road, but in open country, where there could be unfenced roads, it is possible to find ponies, deer, sheep and cattle roaming free. Remember, vehicular traffic must give priority to animals on the road unless so doing might endanger human life.

13

GIVE WAY TO TRAINS!

The Highway Code gives a set of rules to help you deal with railway level crossings and tramways. They are very informative, and deserve your undivided attention to what you need to know. You might notice that yellow box junction markings have been painted on some railway crossings. This should not be necessary if the rules here are followed. However, it does highlight the need to keep the rails and the area within the crossing barriers clear.

The splendid title of this short chapter reflects a piece of advice regrettably now removed from the Highway Code. When a train and a road vehicle collide, the train [always] wins. Likewise, trams are unforgiving too; give way to them. Remember they approach fast – and quietly. They also have their own signals and you should take care not to act on **them** by mistake.

14

NATIONAL AND VEHICLE SPEED LIMITS

The Highway Code shows a grid with different types of vehicles and the speed limits which are applied to them on different types of road. Needless to say, you should always know what restrictions apply to the vehicle you are driving, and it often helps to know what restrictions apply to other vehicles too. This is why your Theory Test may contain specific questions about any of these limits.

For learning purposes you can group various types of vehicle together in order to simplify the grid, e.g. coaches and smaller goods vehicles share the same restrictions except for a special one on motorways. All vehicles are limited to 30 mph in built-up areas and so on.

15

SIGNALS

General information on traffic light signals and their sequences are covered in the Highway Code. Only two things to add here, both being things which are frequently done by mistake. The driver who does them usually thinks he is correct, whilst in fact, he is wrong and potentially dangerous if another vehicle is following his.

The first happens when there is **no** red traffic light on a filter to the right, to hold traffic at the Stop line (see fig 23A).

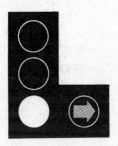

Fig 23(A)

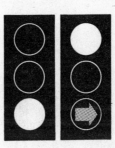

Fig 23(B)

If when the main lights are green for you it is safe to proceed as far as the normal right turn waiting position at the centre of the road, you should move there, even though the filter arrow may not yet be lit. This is because some traffic lights are set up so that sensors (at the turning point) determine whether the filter light should operate or not. If, instead of moving forward as just described, you wait at the Stop line you will not trip the sensor and the filter light will not operate. The main lights will change through their normal sequence back to red, and you will have to stay where you are at the Stop line. You will have missed your turn. (If you were moving up to the Stop line when the main green light was showing, and you decided to wait at the line, I can almost guarantee that the driver behind you would be expecting you to go on to the turning position. Unless he was wide awake you would be at risk of being bumped . . .)

Where there is no oncoming traffic for which you would **have to wait** in the normal right turn waiting position, you need not wait for the green filter arrow to come on; just complete your turn.

If there **is** oncoming traffic, simply wait for the green filter to come on to allow you to complete your turn. During this special, additional phase, oncoming traffic will have been made to stop at red.

Where there **is** a red traffic light to hold the right turn lane at the Stop line (see fig 23B) however, the sensors are at the Stop line. Don't move beyond it until your green filter arrow shows you can.

The second mistake usually happens when a driver has started to turn right, then sees and stops at the red light which is holding back the traffic coming from his original left (see fig 24).

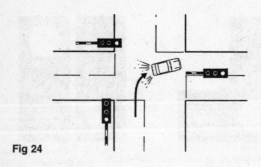

Fig 24

This recipe for a tail-end shunt is a known problem. Traffic engineers are trying to eradicate it by fixing vanes to lights where this problem is particularly bad. These make it difficult to see which light is lit except when driving from the appropriate direction.

The Highway Code shows the various arm signals which traffic controllers will use in order to direct traffic. Remember, the **STOP** signals **MUST** be obeyed. The beckoning signals should also be obeyed but occasionally mistakes are made. If the controller waves you into danger, it is ultimately your responsibility to decide if it is safe to proceed.

The Code says direction indicators and brake-light signals

should only be used for the purposes described. I just wish it said that, for the purposes described, they '*must*' be used.

The Highway Code then shows you the various arm signals which you should use in order to make your intentions clear. These signals are needed if your vehicle either has no electric indicators, or if a fuse blows rendering them inactive, or if you need to reinforce your indicated signal; something you should do, for example, if you are aware that bright sun could be preventing your indicator being seen. Remember, these signals cannot be given adequately with your hand alone, for example: the difference between the slowing down and turning left arm signals becomes almost impossible to see. Therefore, for unmistakable clarity your full arm must be used. There are still some vehicles around which do not have indicators, and you need to know what their drivers are signalling to you.

Please note. There is no driving signal which consists of only one or two raised fingers!

16

ROAD SIGNS

Traffic signs, along with road markings, help you to anticipate hazards ahead and the likely actions of other road users.

Without road markings, no-one would know who has priority at junctions etc. Without traffic signs the speed restrictions, instructions, warnings of dangers ahead, and the necessary information with which you navigate, would all be missing. The last time this situation existed, each motor vehicle had to be preceded by a man walking with a red flag.

So, what I am suggesting is that we treat knowledge of traffic signs and road markings as essential. By knowledge, I do not mean just learning the Highway Code description, but what each sign really means and how to take advantage of the information each sign or marking gives us. For example, knowing where you are likely to see a sign makes it easier to understand what it is telling you.

A number of the following signs are gradually being replaced by up-to-date versions which are easier to understand. I have concentrated my analysis on the 'old' signs, because you will still find them in common use on the road.

There are three basic shapes of traffic sign:

Circles – which give orders and must be obeyed.
Triangles – which warn you of what is ahead.
Rectangles – which give you information.

Circular Signs
There are two basic circular types: red and blue. The red ones are generally restrictive and tell you things that are not allowed. Blue signs tell you things which **MUST** be complied with. For easy reference I have given each sign in this book its own number.

Sign no. 1 says that you are **not allowed** to drive faster than 40 miles per hour.

1. (red circle, black figures, white background)
2. (red circle, white background)
3. (white arrow, blue background)
4. (white arrow, blue background)
5. (white arrow, blue background)
6. (white background, red circle, black wording, black figures)
7. (white background; top: red circle, black figures; bottom: grey circle, grey figures)
8. (black diagonal, white background)

The authorities will have assessed the safe speed for this particular section of road and decided that the criteria present make this road suitable for a 40 mph **maximum** limit. This limit remains in force until you pass a sign which changes it to another speed. Do not believe the 'experts' who tell you that you are allowed to exceed this by 10%, i.e. 44 mph. This would not only be illegal, but dangerous.

Sign no. 2 says that **no vehicles are allowed** past this point. It means **no vehicles**. If it meant something else, there would be a different sign.

No. 3 orders that you **MUST** go straight ahead.

It usually means no other route is available to you. It should not be confused with the sign for a one-way street, which is rectangular (see no. 4) also compulsory, and therefore included in the Highway Code on the same page as the blue circular signs.

No. 5 orders you to keep left of it at traffic islands, road works etc., and places where it is necessary for you to keep to the left. You will also see the keep right version sometimes.

I shall come back to the remaining blue signs later, but for now we'll continue with the red ones.

No. 6 shows the entry to a section of road which has been assessed as being dangerous enough to warrant a speed limit of 20 mph.

This can be for various reasons, but often because the roads concerned – such as those on a housing estate – may have children playing or because there is a large presence of pedestrians or simply to stop traffic using a particular route as a 'Rat Run' to avoid delays on main roads. These limited speed zones often include traffic-calming measures, such as speed humps (also known as 'sleeping policemen').

Failure to slow down for such measures is not just a matter of breaking the law. If you drive over a speed hump too fast, you are likely to lose proper control of your vehicle and will possibly cause a fair amount of damage to your suspension, exhaust and body-work.

No. 7 shows the end of such a restriction, where the speed limit returns to the standard 30 mph for built-up areas.

A "built-up area" is defined as a place where there is normal street lighting. It has nothing to do with buildings, the amount of traffic, or the number of traffic lanes on the road. Therefore, if there is normal street lighting, with lamp-posts less than 185 metres apart, and there is not a sign to say otherwise, the speed limit is 30 mph.

No. 8 shows where the National Speed limit begins. Although not contained in a red circle, it is on the red circle page of the Highway Code because it is still a restrictive sign. It shows the end of a lower speed restriction, but is also to remind you that the national maximum speed limit is applied to the next section of road. The limit for that section will depend on the vehicle you are driving and what type of road it is, i.e. single or dual carriageway, motorway, etc.

Many drivers are annoyed when delayed by slower moving vehicles when, in fact, the other driver may well be applying the correct speed restriction for his circumstances. Knowledge of the various limits is essential if you wish to avoid being unnecessarily stressed. (See Chapter 14.)

Remember, a dual carriageway is where there is some form of (mostly continuous) separation between the traffic travelling in opposite directions. This can range from a strip of crash barrier to a field of crops, each direction of traffic having its own carriageway. A single-carriageway road is where traffic travelling in both directions uses the same road surface, and is only separated by road markings and traffic islands. Both single and dual-carriageway roads may have single or multiple lanes in each direction.

Next we come to a list of signs which just say **NO**. Most of these are self-explanatory, though some could use a little extra help.

Sign 9 means No Entry. You cannot take a vehicle past this point. It is probably showing you the **out** end of a one-way street, or the exit of a car park.

No. 10 tells you that you cannot turn right at this point. It is seen in places where to do so would either interrupt the flow of traffic coming from the opposite direction, or where waiting in a suitable position to turn right would hamper others. It is also used to stop you turning into a No Entry road.

No. 11 shows places where you are not allowed to turn left. Often this is to stop you entering a one-way street in the wrong direction, but sometimes it is purely to stop you making a difficult turn into a narrow road.

9   10   11   12

13   14   15   16

9. (white horizontal, red background)
10. (red circle, red diagonal over black symbol, white background)
11. (red circle, red diagonal over black symbol, white background)
12. (red circle, red diagonal over black inverted U, white background)
13. (red circle, black car on left, red car on right, white background)
14. (red circle, black vehicles, white background)
15. (red circle, black car, white background)
16. (red circle, black bus, white background)

Sign 12 prohibits U-turns in this section of road, usually because the road is too busy for such a manoeuvre to be safe. Do not presume that a failed U-turn (which becomes a three-point-turn) would be allowed either. This sign also bans those.

Sign 13 means No Overtaking. This will be shown in places where to overtake would be particularly dangerous, such as on narrow roads with little forward vision or lots of bends. This restriction remains in force until you reach an identical sign with an end plate (sign 29) fixed underneath, which cancels the restriction.

No. 14 means no motor vehicles. You could take your horse-and-cart or bicycle past this sign, but not your moped.

No. 15 is a bit less restrictive. You can take your moped, scooter or motorcycle past this one but not your car or any larger vehicle.

No. 16 is designed to stop 'casual' visits by coaches and mini-buses with more than 8 seats. Scheduled services, school and works' buses are allowed provided a qualifying sign (see sign 31) is attached.

No. 17 means no cycles. This is usually to be found at the end of pathways and pedestrian areas and is probably one of the most ignored signs in the Code after the speed limit signs.

No. 18 means no pedestrians. This is often found at the entrance to tunnels or at the beginning of bridges, or anywhere it would be dangerous for people on foot. Beware, pedestrians often disobey it.

Signs 19-24 prohibit vehicles of carrying capacity, length, height, width or weight borne on one axle, greater than figures shown by each individual sign, from passing them. These signs have many uses, for example, to prevent drivers of large vehicles

17. (red circle, black bicycle, white background)
18. (red circle, black silhouette, white background)
19. (red circle, black lorry, white background)
20. (red circle, black lorry, white background)
21. (red circle, black measurements and triangles, white background)
22. (red circle, black measurements and triangles, white background)
23. (red circle, black measurement and symbol, white background)
24. (top: black wording, white background; bottom: grey background outside red circle with black wording and black figures on white background)

taking short cuts through unsuitable roads which might be narrow and possibly further restricted by parked cars, or where a restricted bridge or high winds might make it difficult, impossible or dangerous. Remember when towing that these restrictions refer to the overall length, width, weight, etc.

25.   (red circle, red diagonals over blue background)
26.   (red circle, black wording, yellow background)
27A. (white wording, red background)
27B. (white wording, green background)

Sign 25 shows the Clearway sign. It means that, unless forced by an emergency or a traffic queue, you are not allowed to stop for any reason. A Clearway may run from one town all the way to the next; however, there will usually be lay-bys provided or properly signed places if you need to pull off the road. These will have appropriate signs to tell you they are there. The restriction remains in force until you reach an identical sign with an end plate (sign 29) fixed underneath. Urban clearways are different and have their own sign (see sign 34).

Hand-held circular signs are no less mandatory than fixed ones.

No. 26 shows the hand-held sign used by School Crossing Patrols (lollipop men and ladies). These people are trained to help children get across the road safely. They try to ensure that the children do not abuse the crossing point and that the approaching motorist is allowed ample time to stop safely. We all know that, despite their efforts, some children are unpredictable. So when you see this sign, be prepared for the unexpected: children not waiting, pushing each other off the kerb or racing across from the other side of the road, etc.

Nos. 27A and 27B show a manual Go-Stop sign. This will usually be found at road works where the width of the remaining road will not allow the traffic to proceed in both directions at the same time. It is operated by workmen who co-ordinate the passing traffic in order to both ensure that the traffic flows and to allow the necessary movements of their works' equipment. If it is a small road works, there may only be one Go-Stop board. If, however, it is an extended road works there may have to be one at each end and, if each end of the operation is out of sight of the other, the workmen may even have to utilise radio in order to co-ordinate their signals. Remember, sometimes mistakes do happen. As at traffic lights, when you have green for go it is still your responsibility to ensure it is safe before you proceed.

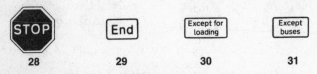

28   29   30   31

28. (white wording, red background)
29. (black wording, white background)
30. (black wording, white background)
31. (black wording, white background)

No. 28 is the *only* octagonal sign. This makes it recognisable even if it is covered in snow. It marks junctions at which you **MUST** stop and is mounted in a permanent position. It will be found where a minor road joins a particularly busy main road, or where the visibility from the minor road is hampered by bends or high walls, etc.

It is designed to make you stop and take full account of the situation in the main road, before deciding when it is safe to proceed further. It will have a corresponding broad white Stop line marked on the road. This is where the front of your vehicle should be whilst you are making your decision. Strictly speaking, if your vehicle stops a couple of feet short of the Stop line, you will not have the best possible view from there. You will also technically be breaking the law if you drive away from that point. You should move up to the line and stop again. Conversely, if you overshoot the line, you are not only breaking the law but risking an accident with, and making life difficult for, the main road traffic.

Qualifying plates are affixed beneath many different signs.

Sign 29 is used to show where restrictions end. The original restriction sign is shown where the restriction is lifted, with this plate attached underneath. An example is explained with sign 25.

Sign 30 typifies an exemption plate on a waiting, parking or access restriction. Loading or off-loading is allowed, though just what constitutes a load is unclear. The task should be completed as quickly as reasonably possible.

Sign 31 is likely to be found attached to the post which is showing sign 16.

Sign 32 exempts vehicles otherwise barred, provided they have a legitimate reason for access. For example, it may be found below sign 14.

Sign 33 means you must have the appropriate permit to park, for which you must apply locally.

Notice on sign 34 that a circular sign, which is similar to the no stopping (Clearway) sign (no. 25) but has only one diagonal line through it, is included in the overall design. As the body of the message tells you, this sign denotes an Urban Clearway. This differs from a Clearway because on these you can stop outside the restricted hours which are displayed on the sign. You may also stop during the restricted hours, but only to set down or pick up passengers.

I have saved no. 35 until last in the red circle set, because it is really half of a pair. It needs to be interpreted in conjunction with sign 111 (rectangular). You will see sign 35 as you reach a narrow road section, bridge or the entrance to a tunnel, etc., where there is insufficient width to allow traffic to pass in both directions at once. It **orders** you to give priority to traffic coming from the opposite direction. Remember it is the **big** (black) **arrow** which has priority and therefore vehicles travelling in the direction of the small (red) arrow must give way. At the other end of the narrowing will be sign 111 showing drivers approaching from that direction that they have priority over your flow of traffic.

No. 36 shows that there is a compulsory turn to the left coming up very soon. It is the **only** way you can proceed from that point. You are most likely to encounter this sign somewhere in a one-way system. Sometimes it is used to show the only direction you can go

32

33

34

35

32. (black wording, white background)
33. (white P on blue square; black wording, white background)
34. (top: yellow background with red circle, red diagonal, blue circle infill, black wording; bottom left: black wording, white background; bottom right: white wording, black background)
35. (red circle, small red arrow, large black arrow, white background)

36

37

38

39

36. (white arrow, blue background)
37. (white arrow, blue background)
38. (white bicycle, blue background)
39. (white bicycle, white figures, blue background)

from a particular lane at traffic lights. There is also a right turn version of this sign.

Sign 37 is telling you that you are about to join a road from the side and **MUST** turn in the direction shown when it is safe to do so. It is quite often accompanied by a qualifying sign stating 'ONE WAY'. This sign is also used to remind you in which direction you **MUST** circulate at roundabouts. (There is a right-handed version of this sign.)

No. 38 labels a route restricted to pedal cycles. These can be helpful to both cyclists and motorists in that they tend to keep them apart. However, cyclists are not obliged to use them and they are still allowed on the rest of the road unless they are specifically barred.

No. 39 depicts places where cycles and pedestrians are sharing a pavement or walk-way which has the appropriate lanes marked on it. In my experience, it is mainly the pedestrians who do not take enough care in the use of these lanes.

Signs 40 and 41 make a pair. No. 40 shows the beginning of a section of road where you are not allowed if you cannot maintain a minimum speed of 30 mph. Sign 41 ends the restriction, which will have been put there to keep slow moving vehicles from using an unsuitable road.

No. 42 shows the sign for a mini-roundabout. These improve traffic circulation and safety as do full-size roundabouts. However, unlike a proper roundabout island, these smaller, kerbless ones are often no more than a slightly domed circle of paint. Normal roundabout rules apply. The positioning of mini-roundabouts in what were previously small junctions means some large vehicles may have to run over the low island in order to negotiate their turns. This is something which needs to be looked for because some of the larger vehicles will not necessarily be in the normal road position for the turn they are executing. If in doubt about how

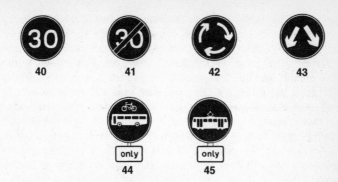

40. (white figures, blue background)
41. (white figures, red diagonal, blue background)
42. (white arrows, blue background)
43. (white arrows, blue background)
44. (top: white vehicles, blue background; bottom: black wording, white background)
45. (top: white vehicle, blue background; bottom: black wording, white background)

much extra room a large vehicle is going to use, always hang back.

Quite often, mini-roundabouts are positioned off to one side, rather than in the middle of the junction. This is done to allow some of the more difficult turns to be negotiated. Please remember this is not done to give priority to traffic from any particular direction.

No. 43 shows a sign which appears on traffic islands, usually in the middle of a one-way street. It means you may pass either side of the island in order to continue your journey in the same direction. There seems to be a lot of confusion about this sign because of what it does **NOT** say. There does not need to be. If there were different destinations to be reached by going down different sides of this island, then they would be sign-posted and marked accordingly.

No. 44 shows a lane that is for the use of buses and cycles **only**. There is another version of this sign which includes taxis. These lanes will be found in the busy parts of town centres and are designed to allow these vehicles to avoid a good deal of the traffic snarl-ups. Of course, having them in a separate lane also stops them from contributing to a lot of the snarl-ups too. Keep a look out in places having these lanes to see if they are only operational at certain times. If this is the case, you are allowed to use them during the non-restricted times. The restricted times are always clearly displayed. This might save you waiting unnecessarily in a queue.

No. 45 specifies a tram lane (the tram tracks should alert you too). It is designed to give the trams their own lane and to facilitate relatively quick journeys for their passengers. Remember, trams move quickly and quietly so never hang about on the tracks. Make sure that if you have to cross the tracks, you will not have to stop on or near them, remembering that the trams themselves are wider than their tracks.

In this same section of the Highway Code are a few rectangular signs which are also coloured blue. Though these are information signs, they are still compulsory and it would be illegal to ignore them.

46   47   48   49

46. (white vehicle, white wording, blue background)
47. (white vehicles, white vertical, blue background)
48. (white vehicle, white arrows, white vertical, blue background)
49. (white bicycle, white vertical, blue background)

Sign 46 shows a defined pedestrian crossing point over the tram tracks. Like any other pedestrian crossing, this is where the tram drivers (and other drivers) should be expecting people to cross over. Because of the amount of view which is restricted by a tram, it is very unwise for pedestrians to cross anywhere else. However, despite the warnings, they do and this, of course, increases the risk of causing an accident.

Sign 47 labels a 'with flow' bus and cycle lane. Only they can use it except in an emergency. Sometimes, these lanes also allow taxis. If you need to cross such a lane in order to take a turning, take extreme care that you do not block the lane. Give way to anyone using it and only cross when you can get completely clear.

Sign 48 labels a 'contra-flow' bus lane, used in places where the traffic is best kept flowing by allowing buses to go the wrong way, in their own lane, against the normal directional flow. You should not use this lane unless there is an emergency, and particular care is needed when crossing such lanes because you must remember to check for buses from their unique direction whilst all the rest of the traffic is flowing the other way. There is a special sign to alert you

and prevent any mistake. This is normally posted facing any traffic
potentially needing to cross such a lane. You can find it among the
Information Signs in your Highway Code.

Sign 49 shows a 'with flow' pedal cycle only lane. If the lane has
a solid line separating it from the other lanes, you are not allowed
in it at all with anything other than a cycle during its period of
operation, except in an emergency. If the lane has a broken line, it
is likely to be in a situation where, although cycles need some
protection from the other traffic, there are not expected to be great
numbers of them. The broken line allows you to use the lane when
it is unavoidable, provided you give priority to cycles. You **MUST
NOT** park on any cycle lane except during its non-restricted hours.

Triangular Signs
Triangular signs warn of hazards ahead. Every one of them
presents information which you should take into consideration
whilst planning the next part of your journey. At the very least, the
sight of a triangular sign should prompt you to check your mirrors
for the up-to-date whereabouts of other vehicles travelling in the
same direction as yourself. This information will prove to be
invaluable if some action is needed for you to negotiate the hazard
ahead. Even if you do not need to take any action, it is a good idea
to know where the other vehicles are anyway.

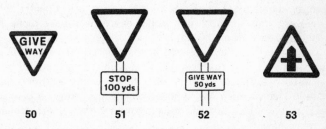

50. (red inverted triangle, black wording, white background)
51. (red inverted triangle, black wording, white background)
52. (red inverted triangle, black wording, white background)
53. (red triangle, black symbol, white background)

Sign 50 is a Give-Way sign. It **MUST** be obeyed. You will
notice that the triangle is inverted (pointing down instead of up).
This is to signify that you are approaching a place (usually a major
road) where it will be necessary to give way. This sign will
normally be accompanied by a Give-Way line (see sign 117) across

the end of your road, showing the place where you will get the best view of the roads ahead. Use this positioning in order to assess whether it is safe to proceed or not. Sometimes there is also an inverted triangle painted on the road just before you reach the line; this reinforces the sign (it is possible to miss the sign in really thick fog).

Signs 51 and 52 show advance warnings of Stop and Give-Way situations ahead. They often have a qualifying sign attached which shows the distance to the junction. They are used where you will not necessarily have a clear view of the situation ahead, e.g. when a major-road junction is round the next bend, or over the brow of a hill. You should be prepared to slow down or stop as necessary.

You may come across many of the following triangular warning signs mounted two, three (or more) on the same post. Logic says the uppermost sign should warn of the first hazard you will reach, with the others in route order down the post, though this is not always to be relied on. Make sure you take in **all** the warnings and then proceed accordingly.

Sign 53 shows advance warning of a crossroads ahead. You can see from the thickness of the lines that you are on the major road (the minor roads will have Give-Way or Stop signs and/or markings) but care needs to be taken in case a vehicle pulls out from one of the minor roads. Often these signs will be placed before junctions where you do not have a clear view of traffic emerging from the minor roads until you are very close to it. Equally, they cannot see your approach any earlier than you can see them. Be prepared to slow down.

Sign 54 warns of a **staggered** junction ahead. The main difference from sign 53 is that any vehicle crossing the major road from one minor road to the other is likely to move into a turning right position (see pages 57/8). It may then have to travel a distance there, before it can turn into the other minor road. Large vehicles

54

55

56

57

54. (red triangle, black symbol, white background)
55. (red triangle, black symbol, white background)
56. (red triangle, black symbol, white background)
57. (red triangle, black symbol, white background)

crossing your path will almost certainly have to move quite slowly to complete these turns. Therefore, the potential for you having to slow down is much increased at this type of junction.

Sign 55 warns about a bend to the right, with a junction to the left on the bend. If you miss the sign, you could well find yourself leaving the major road at the junction, without giving the appropriate signal! Apart from telling you the new direction of the major road, this sign is meant to warn you that the junction will be doubly tricky in view of the limited vision both you and the other motorists have.

Sign 56 shows advance warning of a junction to the left where the major road is going to bend **sharply** to the right. Special care should be taken to watch for traffic coming from, or crossing your path into, the minor road (on your left) because the driver, having misunderstood the junction layout, thinks he has priority over you.

Sign 57 warns of a sharp right-hand bend. It should make you assess your speed and adjust it, if necessary, to a speed which will enable you to negotiate the bend safely. If a tree has fallen just around the bend you must be able to stop. Recognise such possibilities before you rush into bends. You should also consider the likelihood of a vehicle approaching the bend from the opposite direction, and the possibility that it might be travelling too fast, or in the wrong road position. Always assume that is the case until you can see it is not. Where possible, you should adjust your road position in order to allow you the best view through the bend. I teach: 'ease it – bend it – squeeze it'. Ease your speed down to the correct speed for the corner, steer appropriately, then accelerate away smoothly. The above also applies when you encounter the left-handed version of this sign. On a left-hand bend you may have the added risk of someone cutting the corner towards you. Again, moderate your speed until such risk is past.

58   59   60   61

58. (white arrows, black background)
59. (red triangle, black symbol, white background)
60. (white wording, red background)
61. (red triangle, black arrows, white background)

Sign 58 (a rectangular one) is used to give extra information on some bends. It emphasises that this is a very sharp bend, and is placed at the sharpest point, showing the direction of the turn. It is also used in other situations, such as on some roundabouts, to emphasise the direction of the flow of traffic.

Sign 59 shows advance warning of a double bend ahead. This example shows that the road bends to the left, then to the right. A mirror image of this is used for bends in the opposite order. These same signs are also used, with a qualifying notice underneath, to signify a series of bends, e.g. FOR 2 MILES, during which you should expect to have to negotiate a number of sharp bends. Again, particular care in the positioning of your vehicle is needed, because of the possibility of a poorly positioned vehicle travelling in the opposite direction.

Sign 60 is another rectangular (information) sign added for emphasis below other signs rather than used alone. It advises you to reduce your speed **now**.

A couple of examples of where you will find this attached to the same post as the warning signs are (a) on the approach to a **very** sharp bend and (b) on the approach to a roundabout on a trunk road (where you could well have got used to travelling at high speed).

Sign 61 gives you advance warning of a roundabout ahead. As well as making you check your mirrors, it should prompt you to start planning which lane, speed, gear, signals, etc., you will need to negotiate your route through the roundabout. There will usually be another sign (rectangular for information) which will indicate the various destinations available, and which exits lead to them. Be prepared to slow down, and stop if necessary, at the Give-Way line.

Sign 62 heralds an uneven surface, not necessarily a roller-coaster stretch of road, but bad enough to affect control of your vehicle unless you are prepared to slow down. Leave a little extra distance between you and the vehicle in front, particularly if it is a two-wheeler.

In extreme circumstances, some roads may be so uneven as to present a danger of long vehicles scraping their undersides on the bumps. Then, sign 63 is used, usually at each end of such a road, to prevent long, low vehicles becoming grounded.

Sign 64 warns that the road ahead is about to narrow, with the right-hand side of the road being restricted in some way. A mirror image shows when the road is narrowing from the left.

Sign 65 warns that the road ahead is going to narrow from both sides.

62   63   64   65

62. (red triangle, black bumps, white background)
63. (red triangle, black symbol, white background)
64. (red triangle, black symbol, white background)
65. (red triangle, black symbol, white background)

Both the above two signs should make you aware that other vehicles may have to change lanes in order to negotiate the narrow section of road. Quite often, either because some motorists spot the signs late, or because they are trying to jump a queue of traffic, you will find drivers leaving their lane change very late and needing to force their way across. Though this can be frustrating, especially if you are being patient in a queue, do not be tempted to try to stop them getting over. This is as dangerous as their action of cutting in.

Road works signs

Road works signs are usually temporary and tend to be set up on the road surface, rather than on posts, so it is not impossible to miss them. Remember, they often have flimsy stands and are frequently blown or knocked over. Special care should be taken when passing through any section of road works. Statistics show a high incidence of accidents at, and approaching, road works.

When you see sign 66, don't expect to see a man struggling with his umbrella ahead – you are being given advance warning of road works.

Fig 25

WHEN RED LIGHT SHOWS WAIT HERE

Often, you will see a sign warning of traffic-light control ahead (see sign 70). Where there are temporary traffic lights set up at road works, there is usually a printed sign (white letters on red background – see fig 25) which tells you where to stop when the red light is showing.

Use the position of this sign as if it had a Stop line painted on the road beside it. That little square thing, seen on the top of some temporary traffic lights, is a sensor. It is directed at the point where the front vehicle in the queue is supposed to stop. If you do not move up sufficiently (or go too far) it is possible that the sensor will not register your presence and the lights may not change in your favour when it should be your turn. Having said all that, make sure that you leave enough room for any large oncoming vehicle to get past your stopping place.

Sometimes, you will find the temporary traffic control is manual. This will comprise of one or more of the road crew, with a large circular sign (see sign 27A and 27B). These signals **MUST** be obeyed.

Special care should be taken at road works with regard to lanes being closed (see sign 104). Look out for the priorities of lanes being altered, and the cones used to temporarily move lane boundaries. Some road works necessitate contra-flow measures. This is where the direction of the normal flow of traffic is reversed. Be sure you take in the details from the advance information signs as you approach. Remember, any temporary speed restrictions **MUST** be obeyed.

66   67   68   69

66. (red triangle, black symbol, white background)
67. (red triangle, black symbol, white background)
68. (red triangle, black arrows, white background)
69. (red triangle, black arrows, white background)

Sign 66 with an END plate (sign 29) shows where the road works finish and the road should be used according to its normal lanes, speed restrictions etc., from there on.

Sign 67 denotes you are approaching the end of a dual carriageway and are about to join a single carriageway. This means a couple of things: (a) the central reservation, which has separated your stream of traffic from the traffic travelling in the opposite direction, is about to disappear; (b) if you are travelling on a section of road where the national speed limit applies, it is going to be reduced by 10 mph.

As you leave the end of the dual carriageway, sign 68 signifies that from that point on traffic travelling in both directions will be using the next section of road (i.e. a single carriageway). Sign 68 is also used to warn you when you are leaving a one-way system and rejoining a two-way section of road.

Where a two-way street crosses a one-way street, you will find sign 69. This is used to warn you that you need to take into account the traffic coming from **both** directions, when you come to the next junction.

70   71   72

70. (red triangle, red, amber and green lights, white background)
71. (red diagonal over red, amber and green lights, black background)
72. (red triangle, black car and symbol, white background)

Sign 70 shows advance warning of traffic lights ahead. This sign will be found where you are close enough to need to start preparing for them (mirrors, speed, road position, etc.) but cannot necessarily see them yet; for example, where the traffic light is round a corner or bend or down in a dip. You will also find this sign whenever traffic lights are used on trunk (national speed limit) roads. In certain places, extra traffic lights (or sometimes it will be Pelican Crossing lights) are placed on very tall poles. I can think of a couple of examples local to where I live, one on a bend and one just over the crest of a hill, where these tall lights alert you to prepare for your arrival at the lights in plenty of time.

Local knowledge can assist you regarding the phasing of traffic lights and crossing signals in your own area; however, common sense can be used on the approach to such places where you do not necessarily know the timing or sequence. For example, if the lights have been at green for a long time during your approach, you should be expecting them to turn amber, then red. If you can see they are red as you approach, they might change to let you through as you reach them, thus saving you an unnecessary stop. You should try to be prepared for every eventuality.

Sign 71, although rectangular, is another sign which gives a warning.

I have put it here, with the traffic lights sign, because it has always struck **me** that it should be in a triangular sign anyway. It is used when the traffic lights you are approaching are out of order.

You should proceed with extreme caution and, where possible, with courtesy. Remember, all the traffic is having to cross Stop lines, so you should **all** be prepared to give way. You will notice that most drivers tend to give way to traffic from their right as at a roundabout. It seems to work quite well provided no one abuses the arrangement, but keep a look out for those who do.

Familiarity breeds contempt
You should be especially careful if there is a change of either the speed of phasing or the priority at traffic signals. (I can think of several places, in the areas that I use most frequently, where traffic signs, speed limits, or the road markings, have been changed recently.)

Since starting to write this book, my tuition car has been involved in an accident caused by the driver of the other car not noticing that a familiar (long-term temporary) traffic light phasing had been changed back to normal working. She had become so used to having extra time on priority whilst turning right at this junction, that she failed to give way to the oncoming traffic (us) which resulted in a collision. Fortunately, no one was hurt, but both vehicles needed extensive and costly repairs.

The moral here is – look at every sign, signal and road marking, even if you drive the same route every day. They may remain the same for years, then one day be changed.

Sign 72 is a tricky warning to interpret. 'If a road is intrinsically slippery, why don't the authorities change the surface?', I hear you ask. Well no, this sign doesn't quite mean that. It means that in certain circumstances, this section of road surface is more likely to be slippery than other sections of road. Perhaps rain water does not drain away from it very well. Perhaps it is an exposed section of road, where the surface temperature drops sharply, due to wind etc., and it is therefore liable to get frosty/icy. Maybe vehicles are always bringing mud onto the road from an adjacent site, and so on. I have also heard a rumour that this sign is used on sections of road which are behind schedule for maintenance (to absolve highway authorities of responsibility?). Think up your own reasons; but be careful, the road is likely to lack the expected amount of grip.

Signs 73 and 74 show advance warnings of a steep hill up and a steep hill down.

These signs used to tell you how steep the hill was by showing the distance up/down you travelled, compared to the distance you

73. (red triangle, black picture, white background)
74. (red triangle, black picture, white background)

travelled along. For example 1 in 10 meant that for every ten units (metres) you travelled forwards on a hill, you gained, or lost, one unit in altitude. The smaller the second number in the equation, the steeper the hill.

Nowadays, the powers that be, in their wisdom, have changed the gradient into a percentage. It might have made more sense in degrees. Anyway, whatever it means, I don't have time to work out how steep a hill is between seeing the sign, and having to tackle the gradient. So I say to myself, 'If it is steep enough to deserve a warning sign, it must be steep enough for me to have to do something about it'. I am therefore thinking, 'mirrors, change down a gear and/or brakes' etc. The lower gear gives greater engine control of downhill speed, thus assisting braking, or enables you better to maintain speed uphill.

75. (red triangle, black silhouettes, black wording, white background)
76. (red triangle, black silhouettes, black wording, white background)
77. (red triangle, black silhouette, white background)

Sign 75 warns of children. It often has a qualifying sign underneath, such as SCHOOL, PLAYGROUND or even PLAY STREET.

Another addition, which is sometimes attached to the same post, is a pair of amber lights, one above the other. When these lights are flashing (alternately) it denotes that a School Crossing is in operation. Usually, the crossing patrol man will switch the lights on when he arrives and switch them off when he has finished seeing the children across. Of course, you should still take extra care here, even if the lights are not flashing, because children will have grown accustomed to using this as their crossing place.

Sign 76 warns about a place where you are likely to find elderly folk crossing the road.

Elderly folk should be given extra time to cross roads. They will not thank me for telling you they are not as quick as they used to be when they were younger, but we will all slow up sometime. I would like to think motorists will give me a little extra consideration when I need it. Don't get impatient if they are slow to get out of your way. Don't rev your engine to try and make them hurry. You are just as likely to give them a funny turn (or worse) by doing that. This sign appears near retirement homes, pension centres and the like. It sometimes has a qualifying plate to indicate the old people may be blind too.

Sign 77 announces a Pedestrian Crossing ahead.

This sign is most often sited in places where you should already be considering your path through the crossing, but maybe cannot see it yet. Some good examples are where the crossing is soon after a bend, or over the crest of a hill.

78. (red triangle, black silhouettes, black wording, white background)
79. (red triangle, black symbol, white background)
80. (red triangle, black symbol, white background)
81. (red triangle, black symbol, white background)

You will notice the characters on sign 78 are facing the traffic, rather than walking across the sign. It warns that you are approaching a stretch of road where there is no footpath, and therefore anyone on foot will be walking (or jogging) in the road.

Bear in mind, that people should walk on the right-hand side of the road. This enables them to see approaching traffic and, if necessary and/or possible, to take appropriate avoiding action. However, keep a look out for those who do not realise that this is the safest way to do it. Also keep a look out for people with youngsters. They might have to walk two abreast (as sign 78 suggests). The same might apply if they are walking animals.

Remember, unaccompanied youngsters may have little sense of danger until it is too late. Accompanied ones sometimes break free too. Be prepared to slow down, or even stop if this proves to be necessary.

Sign 79 provides advance warning of a cycle route ahead. (Blue signs 38 and 49 label the lanes themselves.) You have to realise that there are fast and slow cyclists. This might necessitate one overtaking another within the cycle lane, and subsequently over-spilling into other traffic lanes. When you see sign 79 you can safely predict that a large proportion of traffic is likely to be cycles, and this may be linked to the time of day, for example, on or near a University Campus. Please remember the emphasis both this book and the Highway Code place on the vulnerability of cyclists.

Sign 80 warns that you are about to join a dual carriageway or motorway from a slip road. You will have to use the slip road whilst deciding whether there is a safe opportunity to move over to your right, and what speed you must attain, in order to merge in safely with the other traffic. It is your responsibility to make this a safe manoeuvre, and it is your stream of traffic which must give way if necessary.

Remember, you must signal your intentions, but this does not mean you can just push your way across. Don't forget to check the blind spot over your right shoulder, just before you move over. If you find that a safe opportunity has not arrived by the time you near the end of the slip road, you will have to be prepared to stop and wait for one. (If you are having to stop, a good tip is to stop a little short of the end; even a short distance will make it much easier to accelerate in, once a gap becomes available. Never attempt to go on by using the hard shoulder as if it were a slip road.) You should make sure that you do not force the other traffic to slow down, stop or move over, in order to accommodate you. Having said that, the other traffic, already on the dual carriageway, will have seen sign 81, and hopefully they will be aware of your needs with regard to this junction.

Remember to take care not to cross continuous white lines whether or not they are infilled with chevrons when you join the dual carriageway or motorway. Follow the markings on the slip road and adjust your speed so that you can merge in smoothly with passing traffic.

The sign 81 warning will be found on dual carriageways on the approach to junctions where traffic will be merging in from your left.

There are four basic courses of action which you can take when you have traffic merging from your left. They all need you to check your mirrors, in order to ascertain where any other vehicles are placed, their relative speeds and any signals they are giving. I am assuming that you are travelling in the near-side (left-hand) lane at, or very near, the speed limit.

Imagine there is a vehicle on the slip road, which needs to merge into your lane and is on a collision course with you unless one of you takes some action.

1. Strictly speaking, it is his responsibility to merge in safely. You could choose to do nothing, and expect him to slow down and merge in after you have passed. Sometimes, due to the volume of traffic on your road, you will have no other choice.
2. Provided you can give following drivers sufficient warning that you are slowing down (with your brake-lights) you could slow down enough to allow the vehicle to merge in front of you.
3. Where option 2 would be dangerous you might (assuming the speed limit will allow and you have some acceleration in hand) be in a position to speed up and leave a gap behind you.

If you choose to use options 2 or 3, try to do so early. If your intentions are not seen clearly by the merging driver, he may slow down or speed up at the same time as you do. This would cancel out the effect of your action.

4. Having checked the other traffic using your road as you approached the slip road and if you consider it to be safe, you could signal, double-check your blind spot and then move over to the lane on your right. This vacates the inner lane which the merging vehicle could then utilise. The fact that you signal, before you move over to your right, will show the merging driver that you are fully aware of his presence and that you are expecting him to merge beside you.

Such helpful considerations are even more important on up-hill stretches of road. Vehicles will be attempting to merge at a speed matching that of the traffic already using the road, but this is not always possible. Some of the heavily loaded trucks may have extreme difficulty in maintaining their momentum if you don't help them. Remember, where you might have to change down a gear to cruise on up a hill, they might have to drop down three or four. With that in mind, whether you are merging or allowing them to merge, try to be considerate if you can. Don't make other drivers slow down unnecessarily.

82 83 84

82. (red triangle, black bridge, white background)
83. (red triangle, black wording, white background)
84. (red triangle, black symbol, white background)

Sign 82 alerts you to a hump-back bridge ahead. This should prompt you to re-check your mirrors and be prepared to slow right down. There are two basic reasons for slowing down. First, if you drive too fast over any hump, there is the possibility that you will lose control of your vehicle and/or take off. Second, any hump in the road will reduce your view of the road beyond it. With a hump bridge, you have no idea what lies beyond until you reach the top of it. The road could be completely clear, but equally, the traffic may be stopped just out of sight. It is not safe to proceed until you know which situation exists. Remember, when you drive over any hump (or round any bend) make sure you can stop well within the distance you can see to be clear.

Sign 83 is a worded warning sign. It could be worded with anything that is not already covered by existing signs, but which drivers need to be warned about. This one doesn't warn you against that make of car! It means that the road is about to cross a river or stream, without the benefit of a bridge. Slow down to walking speed or less so that you will not swamp your engine or anyone else's, nor soak some unsuspecting pedestrian. Immediately you have left the water, having checked in your mirror it is safe to do so, test that your brakes are functioning properly. If they are not, give them a chance to dry out before you proceed with the rest of your journey.

There is a method which can be used to help your brakes dry out quickly, but this must be used very cautiously. I would suggest you try to do this when your brakes are working normally and somewhere safe (like in an empty car park) before you actually need to use it in earnest. Having checked there is no vehicle immediately following yours, put the car in first gear and drive off slowly, then **very gently** apply the foot brake with your left foot whilst still keeping a little pressure on the accelerator. The first time you try this you will probably overdo the brake because your left foot has been conditioned to taking the clutch pedal up and down the full distance. However, doing this with wet brakes will restore their normal stopping power in a very short distance because it heats the brakes and disperses the water.

Sign 84 warns you of loose chippings on the road. The danger here is not merely that other vehicles might flick stones up and damage your paint or windscreen. The sign also warns that you may not have perfect grip between your tyres and the road surface. Any sharp acceleration, braking, or steering is likely to trigger a skid. Never exceed any advisory speed limit shown with this sign while the surface is still loose.

Level Crossing signs

There are three basic signs which warn you about railway level crossings as you approach.

85   86   87   88

85. (red triangle, black gate, white background)
86. (red triangle, black steam train, white background)
87. (red borders, white background)
88. (above: two red lights above a yellow light, black background; below: black wording, white background)

Sign 85 warns you are approaching a crossing with barriers or gates, which will block the road when trains are about to cross your path. Where a level crossing is concealed (perhaps round the next bend) there can also be countdown markers (explained with sign 115) in place too. These should help you to gauge how far you are from the crossing in order to prepare early.

Signs 86 and 87 warn of a railway crossing ahead which has

neither barriers nor gates. These open crossings must be treated with the greatest of respect. Trains should sound their horns, whistles or two-tones as they approach, but you may not hear this above background noises such as wind, stereo or conversation, etc. Always stop before you cross, unless or until a sufficient view both ways confirms you can cross the railway safely. Remember, there could be more than one train, so check carefully before proceeding.

If there are only half-barriers, **never** be tempted to wriggle round them when they are down. Do not take chances. Trains cannot stop as quickly as a car, and they can be moving faster than you think. Every year we hear news reports of trains hitting vehicles on crossings (more than sixty in one recent year). Don't become one of these dreadful statistics.

Sign 88 gives advance warning of railway level crossing light signals ahead. This sign is often used in conjunction with others, such as sign 85. If a train is approaching the crossing, the lights – mounted at the crossing barrier itself – will be activated. First a steady amber light will show, accompanied by a loud alarm (either bells or screech horn) for a very short period; the barriers will then descend and the red lights will take over from the yellow and flash alternately. This light-alarm-barrier sequence is triggered by an approaching train (maybe going flat-out). Once it has been started, it is irreversible – a train **will** arrive. **Never** be tempted to abuse the laid down procedures. Make sure you understand the sequence and could act accordingly if necessary.

You should stop before the crossing when the amber light shows, unless you have already started across. You should be approaching (having seen the sign) carefully enough for that to be possible. The red lights continue to flash until the barriers are lifted. Remember, if the lights continue to flash after the train has passed there is another train coming.

Sign 88, followed by these special lights/alarm, can be found in lots of other interesting places. On the approach to opening type bridges, fire and ambulance stations, even places where a stretch of road has to be temporarily closed for a few minutes at a time. One example of this is at Bristol Airport. There the planes have to fly so low over the road when they are coming in to land that the road (A38) has to be closed for safety reasons each time it happens. Incidentally, it is a spectacular sight when they fly past if you are at the front of the queue.

Sign 89 warns that you can suddenly expect to see (and/or hear) low-flying aircraft. Avoid looking for them and at them – concen-

89. (red triangle, black aeroplane, white background)
90. (red triangle, black tram, white background)

trate on the road. I can assure you that some other idiot will be looking at them when he should be concentrating on his driving, and this could prove to be dangerous for you if you are not alert. I'm not saying you can't go plane spotting, but 'not while you are driving!'

Sign 90 warns that you are about to cross paths with a tram line. Remember – always give way to trams. You should make sure that you are going to be able to get right across, and do not proceed if you are going to have to stop, blocking the line.

91. (red triangle, black deer, white background)
92. (red triangle, black horse, white background)
93. (red triangle, black horse and rider, white background)
94. (red triangle, black bull, white background)

Sign 91 warns of the likelihood of finding wild animals, such as deer, on the road. This happened to me one night as I was driving at about 40 mph through part of the New Forest with a clear road ahead. Suddenly, five or six deer leapt over the fencing on my left, dashed across the road just in front of me, leapt the fencing to my right and were gone. The whole incident lasted no more than two or three seconds. Fortunately sign 91, seen earlier, had prompted me to restrain my speed. Had I not been half expecting this to happen, I doubt that I would have been able to react quickly enough to avoid them.

Sign 92 warns that wild horses or ponies are free to roam. These tend to be less wary of the traffic. Sometimes, they even seem to be contemptuous of it. They often stand in the road and only move out of your way when they feel like it. Remember, it is their home, their natural habitat. We are the visitors. Be patient and enjoy seeing them, rather than risk injuring them by rushing past. Do not make any loud noises near horses; this could spook them into some dangerous reaction.

Sign 93 gives you advance warning of the likelihood of finding horse riders on the road ahead. Expect a bridle-path, crossing or alongside the road, or riding stables situated nearby. As above you should take special care when you have to pass horses. Give them as much room as you safely can. Do nothing suddenly. Above all, pass them quietly.

Sign 94 warns that there could be cattle on the road ahead. We have little choice but to allow cattle on the road priority over vehicular traffic. Except for roads which pass over cattle grids, which could mean you will find cattle roaming freely, most cattle on the road will be accompanied by their handlers. They (the cattle) tend to be slow movers, so don't expect them to hurry out of your path. Be patient, be prepared to stop if necessary and, as with horses, pass them quietly.

95.   96   97

95. (red triangle, black symbol, white background)
96. (red triangle, black lifting bridge, white background)
97. (red triangle, black rocks, white background)

Sign 95. Quayside or Riverbank. This has one of the oldest jokes in the book attached to it. I can almost guarantee that if I ask any of my pupils (who has a sense of humour) what it means, they will reply, 'Dip your headlights'.

However, it does have its serious side. Most drivers believe it means the river or quayside runs along beside the road, and that there may be no kerb or wall to stop you driving straight into the water. There is more to it than that though. When I see this sign by a river, I start to look out for people sitting on fishing stools, their equipment and rods beside them, etc. I look for vehicles with dinghies on trailers, or inflatables on their roof-racks, etc. Whilst people are manhandling boats they are not necessarily keeping as good an eye on the traffic as they should be. If it is a quayside, I am looking for the hoists or cranes lifting the fish boxes from the boats, and the trucks waiting for the boxes maybe jockeying for position, etc. In short, I look for the type of people and things my experience tells me are likely to be there.

An opening bridge will have sign 96 to announce it. You should be prepared for it to be operating. Local radio is a good way to find out when these bridges are going to be opening. If you have this information, you can plan your journey accordingly. In the final stages of your approach to the bridge, look out for drivers racing to get across before it opens. Equally, beware of drivers who, having been held up at the bridge, may now be racing towards you, desperately trying to make up time. Plan to allow extra time for your journey just in case you are held up, and don't be tempted to join the racing if you are.

Sign 97 firstly alerts you to look out for rocks which may be tumbling down or which have already landed on the road. Secondly, it should prompt you to think what oncoming traffic may suddenly have to do by way of avoiding action. The presence of any loose material on the road should sound alarm bells – there might be more obstructions ahead. Fortunately, serious problems are reasonably rare.

98   99

98. (red triangle, black measurement and triangles on white background, white width indication)
99. (red triangle, black electricity symbol, black wording, white background)

Sign 98. This sign is an interesting one. Not only is there a triangular sign (which can also be displayed on its own, somewhere before you reach the obstacle) but also an indication of how wide the available height is. You will notice the triangles in the sign are not of equal size (unlike sign 21). This indicates that there is something physical (e.g. a bridge) which is restricting the available height. Most drivers do not immediately realise that this is relevant to them if they are only driving a small vehicle.

However, if there is a large (high) vehicle coming from the opposite direction it will need to use the highest part of the clearance available, usually in the middle of the road. Be prepared to look through the bridge/tunnel before you attempt to drive through. If there is a large vehicle coming from the opposite direction, be ready to wait.

Sign 99 warns that there are power cables overhead, and that it is not safe to proceed if your vehicle or any part of your load is higher than the stated measurement. Touching or even getting close to high voltage power cables is extremely undesirable.

Sign 100 shows the distance to a tunnel entrance. You will also (hopefully) know whether your vehicle can go through or not, and whether this is the route you want to take. If you are not intending to go through the tunnel, this sign warns you how much distance you have in which to find a suitable place to turn back.

Sign 101 warns you that there are traffic calming measures ahead. These are designed to slow vehicular traffic down to a safe speed for the circumstances ahead. Humps are not the only means of slowing traffic down, so keep a look out for combinations of the different types. Sometimes, a deliberate narrowing of the road is

100
101
102
103

104

100. (red triangle, black tunnel, black wording, white background)
101. (red triangle, black hump, black wording, white background)
102. (red triangle, black exclamation mark, black wording, white background)
103. (black border, black picture, yellow background)
104. (black border, two black arrows, one black vertical line topped with red horizontal line, yellow background)

used, perhaps incorporating a chicane or zig-zag. Rumble strips across the road or, sometimes, a stretch of particularly noisy road surface are also used. To state the obvious, if it sounds or feels unsafe, you are probably driving too fast. Be prepared to slow down and keep your eyes peeled for the root cause of the traffic calming measures, e.g. old people, schools, children, etc.

Sign 102 shows an exclamation mark'!'. It warns of danger ahead. It says 'there is a surprise coming up, but we don't have an exclusive sign for it'. It should make you think 'what?'. Most of these signs have a qualifying plate underneath to tell you what the danger is, but not all. When you see this sign you should be prepared to look further ahead than you do normally. The object of this sign is to make you aware of something which is out of the ordinary.

A good example of this exists on a busy (70 mph) dual carriageway I know. There is a pub and petrol station combination, each with its own car park beside it. However, the slowing down lane for entering these two properties is only about thirty metres long. This causes vehicles to slow down considerably whilst they are still in the nearside lane of the normal carriageway, before entering the slip lane. Perhaps it is understandable that they cannot design a sign to give us those details, so this '!' sign has been used to alert you to danger ahead.

Sign 103 is probably included with the triangular signs because it gives a warning as well as information. You will see this sign in the back (and sometimes front or side) windows of school buses. It is designed to make you aware of the possibility that children could be either boarding or alighting from the bus. Special care is required whenever you pass a stationary bus bearing this sign. It is advisable to look out for any passengers, adult or otherwise, whenever you drive past a stationary bus.

Rectangular Signs

Rectangular signs give you information. They can include directions and temporary road works details, such as closed lanes (sign 104) amongst many other things. Most are self explanatory though some explanation here may be useful.

Information signs on motorways have a blue background, with a white edge. For example, sign 105 shows the number of the exit junction you are approaching, where it leads to, and the destinations available to you further along the motorway.

Where the information sign is on an A-Class road (primary

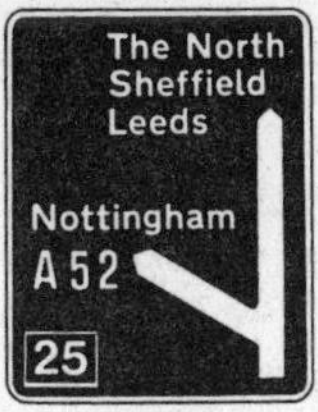

105

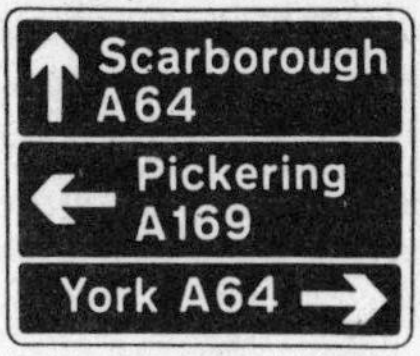

106

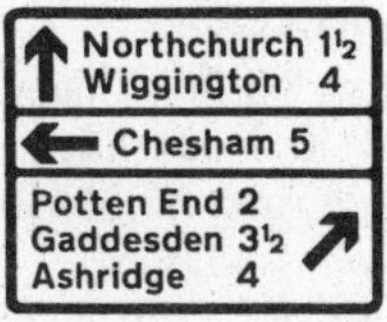

107

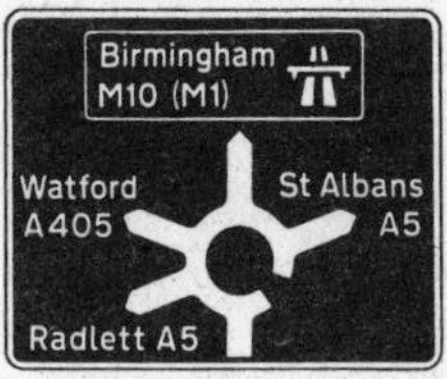

108

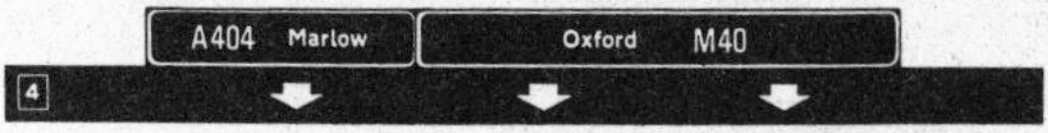

109

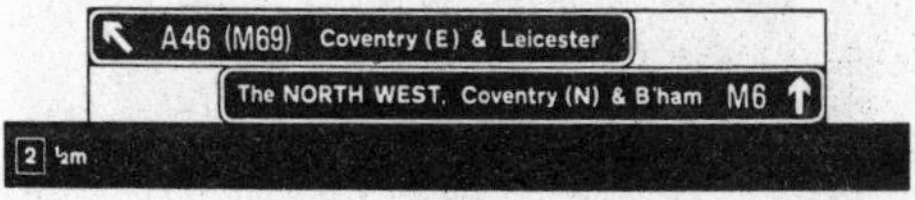

110

105. (white wording, white lines, small black junction number square in bottom left, blue background)
106. (white place names, yellow road numbers, white arrows, green background)
107. (black wording, black arrows, white background)
108. (main panel: white place names, white symbol, yellow road numbers, green background; top panel: white wording, white motorway symbol, blue background)
109. (top: white wording, blue background; bottom: white junction number, white arrows on blue backgrounds, overall black background)
110. (top two panels: white wording, white arrows, blue background; bottom panel: white junction number on black background, white distance indicator on blue background, general black background)

route), the background will be green with a white edge (sign 106).

Those on a B-Class road (non-primary route) have white backgrounds and black edges (sign 107).

Colour coding is particularly helpful when you have a combination of types of road to choose from, as in sign 108. Here, for example, learner drivers would not be allowed to take the straight ahead exit.

Over-head signs such as 109 and 110 give **more** details than the basic information regarding destinations. These signs can be used to show turn-offs from motorways and by-passes.

Sign 109 tells you that in order to turn off for Marlow, all you have to do is get into the left-hand lane and stay there. This lane will be splitting off to become a separate road (to Marlow) whilst the other two lanes will continue on towards Oxford.

Sign 110 shows that in order to turn off for Coventry (E) & Leicester you will not only have to get into the left-hand lane, but will have to look out for the exit road and its markings. These will lead you into a deceleration lane which will probably end up at a

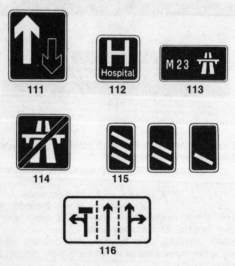

111. (large white arrow, small red arrow, blue background)
112. (white wording, blue background)
113. (white wording, white motorway symbol, blue background)
114. (red diagonal over white motorway symbol, blue background)
115. (white diagonal bars, blue backgrounds)
116. (red horizontal line on left, black arrows, white background)

roundabout, which you will have to negotiate in order to get onto the correct road for your destination.

Sign 111 informs of **your** priority over oncoming traffic as you pass through a narrow section. Oncoming traffic must give way. As with sign 35, it is the **large arrow** which indicates the **priority**.

Sign 112 shows a Hospital ahead. To me, it also warns: look out for ambulances – look out for people who might not be concentrating on the traffic due to grief, drugs, etc., etc. Hospital vicinities are areas for driving carefully and quietly too.

Signs 113 and 114 mark the start and end of a motorway respectively. Sign 113 is repeated at every entry point. If any restriction prohibits you or your vehicle from motorways you **MUST NOT** pass this sign. Advance warnings of motorway routes ahead are often shown in signs like 108.

Sign 115 shows countdown markers. These are used to inform you of the distance to the next turn-off, roundabout, etc. They are spaced at standardised (and therefore memorable) intervals. Those shown are blue-backed, which signifies that they are on a motorway, showing an exit. If the signs had green backing, they would be on a major route (A road) and could show either a turn-off or a roundabout. Sometimes, roundabouts on non-primary routes (B roads) are also labelled with countdown markers, and where this happens, the sign usually has a white backing with black bars. If you see countdown markers showing **red** bars on a white background, these will indicate that you are approaching a railway level crossing.

The idea of having these markers on the approach roads is to assist you with your deceleration. Often, after driving on a fast road for any length of time, it can be quite difficult to judge accurately the amount of road you will need in order to slow down safely. You can also use the countdown markers as an indication of the correct place to start signalling, if there is a turn-off involved or a roundabout to negotiate. When you are travelling at 60/70 mph, the three bars marker is the place to start showing others that you intend to take an exit (by indicating) or to begin to slow down for the roundabout (by brake-lights).

Sign 116 shows which lane you should use in order to reach your intended destination. You will find this sign in places where the volume of traffic means you cannot always see the appropriate road markings, and especially where you are required to use unusual lanes to reach your destination, i.e. the left lane to turn right, or the right lane to go straight ahead at a roundabout.

Stopping Lines – across the road

Where these lines are to be found and how to interpret them is explained in Chapter 8.

This section starts with sign 117, the type of white Give-Way line found at junctions into major roads.

This shows the point where you should assess the safety of joining the major road. Remember, the rule you should apply when joining traffic from a Stop or Give-Way line is: do **not** pull out if your action would cause any other vehicle to slow down, stop, or move over.

No. 118 is the white Give-Way line for a roundabout. You must give way to vehicles coming from your right.

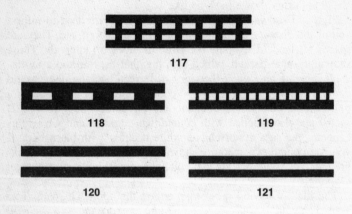

No. 119 is the white line used at mini-roundabouts. Often, mini-roundabouts have been added as an afterthought to a junction where some roads are larger or busier than others. Remember, just because your road may be busier, it does not necessarily have priority. The rule remains: give way to traffic from your right, however occasionally it may apply.

No. 120 is the white **STOP** line, found at junctions where the authorities consider it would be too dangerous if drivers were given the choice about whether or not to stop. Remember, you are expected to get the front of your vehicle right up to the line and stop there, before you make your decision about the safety of pulling out.

No. 121 is the thinner type of white Stop line you will find at traffic lights. It marks the place where the vehicle at the front of the waiting traffic should stop.

Take care when you stop at or move up to any of the above lines, to position your vehicle with its front *at the line*. There is nothing to be gained by overshooting the line. In fact, by doing so, you might put yourself in a position where you are unable to see any traffic signals which are present. However, stopping short often prevents you getting the best view.

In order to assist drivers in judging their speed of approach, some dangerous junctions and high speed approaches to roundabouts are marked with yellow bands across the road. The distance between the bands decreases as you get nearer to the give-way or stop lines. If you do not slow down sufficiently, the lines flashing past under your wheels give the illusion that you are actually speeding up and create the natural urge for you to slow down. (Good psychology eh?)

Another psychological tool employed to make you slow down can often be found where a country road enters a village. Here you will sometimes see a sign asking you to drive carefully through the village, and a 'thank you' sign is often erected where you leave it. In some places, as you approach such villages, you will drive over a section of road which is brightly coloured (red, pink, orange, green, etc.), which also produces a rumble effect as your tyres go over it. The message is the same – slow down and be alert.

Waiting and loading restrictions

The Highway Code section dealing with waiting restrictions needs no further explanation. Always make sure that if you need to wait or park, it is both legal and safe to do so. Try to be considerate, even when you are legally parked. Watch out when opening doors on a stationary vehicle. Pedestrians and cyclists usually come off worst if your door hits them. Look in the Information signs section of the Highway Code for controlled parking zone signs – which you also need to be able to recognise.

Miscellaneous road markings

You should keep a special look out when in the vicinity of schools. Where there are yellow zig-zag markings along the edge of the road (no. 122) with or without the words 'SCHOOL-KEEP-CLEAR', this designates a stretch of road which **MUST** be KEPT CLEAR.

It **DOES NOT** mark out a space where parents are allowed to

122

stop in order to drop their children outside the school. The idea of keeping this area clear is to give passing motorists the maximum field of view.

You should always be thinking about the unpredictability of children, particularly if they are either playing or hurrying somewhere. Never think of turning round in the road on or near these markings.

The other road markings shown in this section of the Highway Code are either self-explanatory, or have already been covered earlier.

Goods vehicle markings are required by law to warn other drivers of potentially dangerous vehicles or loads. Some of these, like the upright right/left-hand side markers, also have to be used on builders' skips, whenever left on the highway. You need to be able to recognise these markings.

The Highway Code also shows the various markings used on vehicles which carry dangerous substances. Hopefully, you will never be involved in an incident with one of these, but should such a thing happen, the emergency services will need to know what is on board in order to deal with the situation properly. There are many reasons why you should always have a pen/pencil and paper in your vehicle and this is just one of them.

The long arm of the law
Finally, just a mention about the law and how you, as a motorist, are affected by it. You need to have certain documentation in order, before you can drive on public highways.

You **MUST** have a signed, in-date, provisional or full driving licence applicable to the vehicle you are driving. Your provisional licence will cover you for learning in both automatic transmission and manually geared cars. However, if you pass your Driving Test in an automatic you will only be qualified to drive automatics. Conversely, if you pass your Test in a manually geared car you will be qualified to drive both types.

You **must** be personally covered by valid third-party insurance for that particular vehicle. (Third party is the **minimum** legal insurance cover; better cover is advisable.)

The vehicle (apart from cars over 25 years old) **must** have a current road fund (road tax) licence displayed on the bottom left-hand corner of its windscreen. You need to show your insurance certificate and MOT certificate – see below – when taxing a vehicle.

If the vehicle is three years old or more (four years in Northern Ireland) it **must** have a current MOT (road worthiness) certificate. (The **only** time you can legally drive such a vehicle without a current MOT certificate is when you are on the way to a pre-booked MOT Test appointment.)

You must be prepared to show your driving licence, the insurance certificate and, if appropriate, the MOT certificate to any police officer who asks to see them. If you are not carrying these documents with you when asked, you could be required to produce them at a police station of your choice within seven days (five days in Northern Ireland). It is an offence if you fail to do this.

Another document you should know about, though not one which has to be produced in most circumstances, is the vehicle registration document. It contains the major details relating to the vehicle, such as make, engine size, keeper's name and address, etc.

If involved in an accident you are **ALWAYS** required to stop. The rest of the law's demands depend on the circumstances regarding damage only, injured persons and so on. A good understanding of what you **must** do is essential *before* you find yourself in an accident situation.

In the event of you being involved in an accident, there are basic items of information which you will need, and you should be prepared to give the same details about yourself to other people involved in the incident. A: Who owns the other vehicle. B: The driver's name, address and telephone number. C: The make and registration number of the other vehicle. D: Details of the other driver's insurance.

To assist you in filling out your report form for insurance or witness statements, it is also advisable to write down details like: exactly where and when the incident occurred; width of road, any signs and/or road markings; speed of the vehicles involved; weather and/or road conditions; which lights and/or indicators were in use, etc.; names and addresses of any witnesses (including people not involved in the incident if possible); any other relevant information. (I sincerely hope you never need this information for any reason other than answering a question in your Theory Test.)

Take care to report the accident if required, as soon as possible and within the time limit.

I do not intend to cover the penalties and consequences for offending the driving laws, nor the vehicle security recommendations made in the Highway Code. However, you might do well to read and consider those details for yourself as at least one question on these subjects is included in the Theory Test Question Bank.

First Aid

I would encourage all drivers to get some knowledge of first aid as the Theory Test puts strong emphasis on this. Failure to acquire enough first aid knowledge could well mean failing the test. I can remember how useless I felt when I had no idea what to do at the scene of an accident. There is some basic advice given in the Highway Code, but personal instruction on a properly recognised first aid course will equip you much better to deal with real emergencies.

One very important thing concerns accidents involving motorcyclists. **Do not** remove the crash helmet from an injured motorcyclist **unless** doing so is essential. You could worsen any hidden injuries.

That completes my analysis of the material for your Driving Theory Test. I hope you have found it to be helpful, not just for that Test but as a foundation for a safe driving future.

17

OFFICIAL QUESTIONS

Now comes the time to try some of the questions, reprinted by kind permission of HMSO and the DSA from the *Official* DSA question bank.

Hopefully, you will not have jumped straight to this section without reading the rest of this book first. Try to answer them without going back to check. Write down your selected answers on a piece of paper, then check them against the answers from page (150) after you have attempted them **all**. Remember, you will only be cheating yourself if you look at the answers first.

I have carefully selected questions from all of the subjects covered by the Theory Test to give you a fair idea of the level of understanding and knowledge required to pass this Test. Against each answer is a page reference from this book to refresh your memory later, in case you experience difficulty.

Q1
To move off safely from a parked position you should
Mark one answer
– signal if other drivers will need to slow down
– use your mirrors and look round for a final check
– NOT look round if there is a parked vehicle close in front of you
– give a hand signal as well as using your indicators

Q2
Which THREE of these emergency services might have blue flashing beacons?
Mark three answers
– Doctors' cars
– Coastguard
– Animal ambulances
– Bomb disposal team
– Gritting lorries
– Mountain rescue

Q3
You see a car showing a flashing green beacon. Should you give way to it?
Mark one answer
- Yes, it is a fire crew support vehicle
- No, it is a breakdown vehicle
- Yes, it is a doctor going to an emergency
- No, it is a slow moving vehicle

Q4
New tyres should be run in at reasonable speeds for the first
Mark one answer
- 10 miles
- 100 miles
- 500 miles
- 1000 miles

Q5
You should ONLY use a hand-held telephone when
Mark one answer
- you have stopped at a safe place
- your vehicle has an automatic gear change
- driving at low speeds
- travelling on minor roads

Q6
A vehicle has a flashing green beacon. What does this mean?
Mark one answer
- The vehicle is slow moving
- A doctor is answering an emergency call
- It is a motorway police patrol vehicle
- A vehicle is carrying hazardous chemicals

Q7
You are following a vehicle on a wet road. You should leave a time gap of at least
Mark one answer
- two seconds
- one second
- four seconds
- three seconds

Q8
The main cause of brake fade is
Mark one answer
- the brakes out of adjustment
- the brakes overheating
- air in the brake fluid
- oil on the brakes

Q9
Driving at 70 mph uses more fuel than driving at 50 mph by up to
Mark one answer
- 10%
- 30%
- 75%
- 100%

Q10
You should ONLY flash your head lamps to other road users
Mark one answer
- to let them know you are there
- to show you are giving way
- to show you are about to reverse
- to tell them you have right of way

Q11
At a pelican crossing the flashing amber light means you should
Mark one answer
- give way to pedestrians waiting to cross
- stop, if you can do so safely
- stop and wait for the green light
- give way to pedestrians already on the crossing

Q12
What should you use your horn for?
Mark one answer
- To alert others to your presence
- To allow you right of way
- To greet other road users
- To signal your annoyance

Q13

A two-second gap between yourself and the car in front is sufficient when conditions are

Q 13

Mark one answer
- foggy
- good
- wet
- damp

Q14

It is essential that tyre pressures are checked regularly. When should this be done?
Mark one answer
- When tyres are hot
- After driving at high speed
- When tyres are cold
- After any lengthy journey

Q15

When must you use dipped headlights during the day?
Mark one answer
- Along narrow streets
- All the time
- When parking
- In poor visibility

Q16

Car passengers MUST wear a seat belt if one is available, unless they are
Mark one answer
- sitting in the rear seat
- exempt for medical reasons
- under 1.5 metres (5 feet) in height
- under 14 years old

Q17
When may you use hazard warning lights?
Mark one answer
- When you have broken down
- To park alongside another car
- To park on double yellow lines
- When you are being towed

Q18
You are carrying two children and their parents in your car. Who is responsible for seeing that the children wear seat belts?
Mark one answer
- The children's parents
- The front seat passenger
- You
- The children

Q19
Hazard warning lights should be used when vehicles are
Mark one answer
- reversing into a side road
- faulty and moving slowly
- being towed along a road
- broken down and causing an obstruction

Q20
You cannot see clearly behind when reversing. What should you do?
Mark one answer
- Ask someone to guide you
- Open your window to look behind
- Open the door and look behind
- Look in the nearside mirror

Q21
The legal minimum depth of tread for car tyres over three quarters of the breadth is
Mark one answer
- 1 mm
- 1.6 mm
- 2.5 mm
- 4 mm

Q22
When approaching a hazard your FIRST reaction should be to
Mark one answer
- check the mirrors
- release the accelerator
- change direction
- use your footbrake

Q23
You wish to park facing DOWNHILL. Which TWO of the following should you do?
Mark three answers
- Turn the steering wheel towards the kerb
- Put the handbrake on firmly
- Park close to the bumper of another car
- Park with two wheels on the kerb
- Turn the steering wheel away from the kerb

Q24
How should you use the emergency telephone on a motorway?
Mark one answer
- Keep your head in the kiosk
- Face the oncoming traffic
- Stay close to the carriageway
- Keep your back to the traffic

Q25
When driving in fog in daylight you should use
Mark one answer
- dipped headlights
- full beam headlights
- hazard lights
- sidelights

Q26
You are at a junction with limited visibility. You should
Mark one answer
- inch forward, looking to the right
- inch forward, looking both ways
- inch forward, looking to the left
- be ready to move off quickly

Q27
You are driving in a built-up area. You approach a speed hump. You should

Q 27

Mark one answer
- move across to the left-hand side of the road
- wait for any pedestrians to cross
- slow your vehicle right down
- stop and check both pavements

Q28
You have driven through a flood. What is the first thing you should do?
Mark one answer
- Switch on your windscreen wipers
- Stop and check the tyres
- Stop and dry the brakes
- Test your brakes

Q29
You are driving in heavy rain when your steering suddenly becomes very light. To get control again you must
Mark one answer
- ease off the accelerator
- use the accelerator gently
- brake firmly to reduce speed
- steer towards a dry part of the road

Q30

How can you tell when you are driving over black ice?
Mark one answer
- The noise from your tyres sounds louder
- It is easier to brake
- You see black ice on the road
- Your steering feels light

Q31

To drive you must be able to read a number plate from what distance?
Mark one answer
- 10 metres (33 feet)
- 20.5 metres (67 feet)
- 205 metres (673 feet)
- 15 metres (49 feet)

Q32

Your doctor has given you a course of medicine. Why should you ask if it is OK to drive?
Mark one answer
- The medicine you take may affect your hearing
- Drugs make you a better driver by quickening your reactions
- Some types of medicine can cause your reactions to slow down
- You will have to let your insurance company know about the medicine

Q33

Which THREE pieces of information are found on a vehicle registration document?
Mark three answers
- Date of the MOT
- Engine size
- Registered keeper
- Service history details
- Make of the vehicle
- Type of insurance cover

Q34

You are involved in a road accident with another driver. Your vehicle is damaged. Which FOUR of the following should you find out?

Mark four answers
- Whether the other driver is licensed to drive
- Whether the driver owns the other vehicle involved
- The other driver's name, address and telephone number
- The occupation of the other driver
- The car make and registration number of the other vehicle
- The details of the other driver's vehicle insurance

Q35

You see a car on the hard shoulder of a motorway with a HELP pennant displayed. This means the driver is most likely to be

Mark one answer
- a foreign visitor
- a disabled person
- first aid trained
- a rescue patrol person

Q36

How often should you stop on a long journey?

Mark one answer
- When you need petrol
- At least every four hours
- When you need to eat
- At least every two hours

Q37

You are about to reverse into a side road. A pedestrian wishes to cross behind you. You should

Mark one answer
- give way to the pedestrian
- wave to the pedestrian to stop
- wave to the pedestrian to cross
- reverse before the pedestrian starts to cross

Q38
What should the driver of the car approaching the crossing do?

Q 38

Mark one answer
- Sound the horn
- Slow and get ready to stop
- Drive through quickly
- Continue at the same speed

Q39
Which age group is most likely to be involved in a road accident?
Mark one answer
- 17 to 25-year-olds
- 36 to 45-year-olds
- 46 to 55-year-olds
- 55-year-olds and over

Q40
You are planning to tow a caravan. Which of these will **mostly** help to aid the vehicle handling?
Mark one answer
- Power steering fitted to the towing vehicle
- A stabiliser fitted to the towbar
- A jockey-wheel fitted to the towbar
- Anti-lock brakes fitted to the towing vehicle

Q41
You are approaching a school crossing patrol. When this sign [red circle, black wording and silhouettes on yellow background] is held up you must

Q 41

Mark one answer
- stop only when the children are actually crossing the road
- stop and beckon the children to cross
- stop and allow any children to cross
- stop only if the children are on a pedestrian crossing

Q42
You are turning left into a side road. Pedestrians are crossing the road near the junction. You must

Q 42

Mark one answer
- wave them on
- sound your horn
- switch on your hazard lights
- wait for them to cross

Q43

You see a pedestrian carrying a white stick. This shows that the person is
Mark one answer
- deaf
- blind
- disabled
- elderly

Q44

A trailer must stay securely hitched-up to the towing vehicle. What additional safety device can be fitted to the trailer braking system?
Mark one answer
- Stabiliser
- Jockey wheel
- Breakaway cable
- Corner steadies

Q45

In which THREE of these situations may you overtake another vehicle on the left?
Mark three answers
- When you are in a one-way street
- When approaching a motorway slip road where you will be turning off
- When the vehicle in front is signalling to turn right
- When a slower vehicle is travelling in the right-hand lane of a dual carriageway
- In slow-moving traffic queues when traffic in the right-hand lane is moving more slowly

Q46

How should you overtake horse riders?
Mark one answer
- Drive up close and overtake as soon as possible
- Use your horn just once to warn them
- Drive slowly and leave plenty of room
- Speed is not important but allow plenty of room

Q47
What is the **maximum** fine when causing death by careless driving whilst under the influence of alcohol?
Mark one answer
- A fine of £500
- A fine of £2000
- A fine of £5000
- An unlimited fine

Q48
You should only use rear fog lights when you cannot see further than about
Mark one answer
- 250 metres (800 feet)
- 200 metres (660 feet)
- 150 metres (495 feet)
- 100 metres (330 feet)

Q49
You are travelling at night. You are dazzled by headlights coming towards you. You should
Mark one answer
- pull down your sun visor
- slow down or stop
- put your hand over your eyes
- switch on your main beam headlights

Q50
To correct a rear-wheel skid you should
Mark one answer
- turn away from it
- turn into it
- not turn at all
- apply your handbrake

Q51

You are driving on a motorway in fog. The left-hand edge of the motorway can be identified by reflective studs. What colour are they?

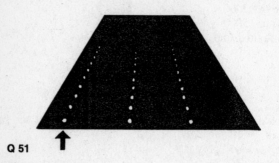

Q 51

Mark one answer
- White
- Amber
- Red
- Green

Q52

You have to park on the road in fog. You should
Mark one answer
- leave sidelights on
- leave dipped headlights and fog lights on
- leave dipped headlights on
- leave main beam headlights on

Q53

You are driving a car on a motorway. Unless signs show otherwise you must NOT exceed
Mark one answer
- 50 mph
- 60 mph
- 70 mph
- 80 mph

Q54
What do these [white on blue background] motorway signs show?

Q 54

Mark one answer
- They are countdown markers to the next exit
- They are countdown markers to a bridge
- They are distance markers to the next telephone
- They warn of a police control ahead

Q55
On a three-lane motorway, which lane should you use for normal driving?
Mark one answer
- Right
- Centre
- Either the right or centre
- Left

Q56
You are driving on a three lane motorway. There are red reflective studs on your left and white ones to your right. Where are you?
Mark one answer
- In the right-hand lane
- In the left-hand lane
- In the middle lane
- On the hard shoulder

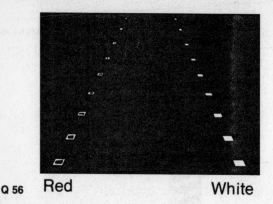

Q 56   **Red**   **White**

Q57
When joining a motorway you must always
Mark one answer
- come to a stop before joining the motorway
- stop at the end of the acceleration lane
- give way to traffic already on the motorway
- use the hard shoulder

Q58
What does this sign [large white arrow, small red arrow, blue background] mean?

Q 58

Mark one answer
- You are entering a one-way street
- You have priority over vehicles from the opposite direction
- No overtaking
- Two-way traffic ahead

Q59
You are driving along a road that has no traffic signs. There are street lights. What is the speed limit?
Mark one answer
- 30 mph
- 20 mph
- 60 mph
- 40 mph

Q60
On a motorway the amber reflective studs can be found between
Mark one answer
- the hard shoulder and the carriageway
- the acceleration lane and the carriageway
- each pair of the lanes
- the central reservation and the carriageway

Q61
What is the legal minimum insurance cover you must have to drive on public roads?
Mark one answer
- Personal injury cover
- Fully comprehensive
- Third party only
- Third party, fire and theft

Q62
You have broken down on an ordinary road. You have a [red] warning triangle. It should be displayed

Q 62

Mark one answer
- at least 150 metres (492 feet) behind your vehicle
- just behind your vehicle
- at least 45 metres (149 feet) behind your vehicle
- on the roof of your vehicle

ANSWERS

A1 *(page 22)*
– use your mirrors and look round for a final check

A2 *(page 38)*
– Coastguard
– Bomb disposal team
– Mountain rescue

A3 *(page 38)*
– Yes, it is a doctor going to an emergency

A4 *(page 15)*
– 100 miles

A5 *(page 20)*
– you have stopped at a safe place

A6 *(page 38)*
– A doctor is answering an emergency call

A7 *(page 29)*
– four seconds

A8 *(page 32)*
– the brakes overheating

A9 *(page 47)*
– 30%

A10 *(page 76)*
– to let them know you are there

A11 *(page 36)*
– give way to pedestrians already on the crossing

A12 *(page 76)*
– To alert others to your presence

A13 *(page 29)*
– good

A14 *(page 14)*
– When tyres are cold

A15 *(pages 33 and 74/5)*
– In poor visibility

A16 *(page 20)*
– exempt for medical reasons

A17 *(page 38)*
– When you have broken down

A18 *(page 20)*
– You

A19 *(page 38)*
– broken down and causing an obstruction

A20 *(page 73)*
– Ask someone to guide you

A21 *(page 14)*
– 1.6 mm

A22 *(page 25)*
– check the mirrors

A23 *(page 77)*
– Turn the steering wheel towards the kerb
– Put the handbrake on firmly

A24 *(page 85)*
– Face the oncoming traffic

A25 *(page 74)*
– dipped headlights

A26 *(creeping and peeping, page 59)*
– inch forward, looking both ways

A27 *(sign 6, page 96)*
– slow your vehicle right down

A28 *(sign 83, page 117)*
– Test your brakes

A29 *(page 30)*
– ease off the accelerator

A30 *(page 29)*
– Your steering feels light

A31 *(page 18)*
– 20.5 metres (67 feet)

A32 *(page 18)*
– Some types of medicine can cause your reactions to slow down

A33 *(page 131)*
– Engine size
– Registered keeper
– Make of the vehicle

A34 *(page 131)*
– Whether the driver owns the other vehicle involved
– The other driver's name, address and telephone number
– The car make and registration number of the other vehicle
– The details of the other driver's vehicle insurance

A35 *(page 85)*
– a disabled person

A36 *(page 82)*
– At least every two hours

A37 *(page 73)*
– give way to the pedestrian

A38 *(page 34)*
– Slow and get ready to stop

A39 *(page 7)*
– 17 to 25-year-olds

A40 *(page 31)*
– A stabiliser fitted to the towbar

A41 *(sign 26)*
– stop and allow any children to cross

A42 *(page 56)*
– wait for them to cross

A43 *(page 34)*
– blind

A44 *(page 31)*
– Breakaway cable

A45 *(page 50)*
– When you are in a one-way street
– When the vehicle in front is signalling to turn right
– In slow-moving traffic queues when traffic in the right-hand lane
  is moving more slowly

A46 *(page 23)*
– Drive slowly and leave plenty of room

A47 *(see Highway Code)*
– An unlimited fine

A48 *(page 74)*
– 100 metres (330 feet)

A49 *(page 75)*
– slow down or stop

A50 *(page 31)*
– turn into it

A51 *(page 43)*
– Red

A52 *(page 78)*
– leave sidelights on

A53 *(Chapter 14)*
– 70 mph

A54 *(sign 115)*
– They are countdown markers to the next exit

A55 *(page 83)*
– Left

A56 *(page 43)*
– In the left-hand lane

A57 *(page 81)*
– give way to traffic already on the motorway

A58 *(sign 111)*
– You have priority over vehicles from the opposite direction

A59 *(page 96)*
– 30 mph

A60 *(page 43)*
– the central reservation and the carriageway

A61 *(page 130)*
– Third party only

A62 *(page 78)*
– at least 45 metres (149 feet) behind your vehicle

I hope you did well with these sample questions. If not, now that you know what level of knowledge you need, try re-reading this book; then try the questions again.

I am probably an idealist, but I think the only way to drive properly is to know your subject inside out, back-to-front and upside down. I think that the more skilled you become, in theory and practice, the safer you become too.

When driving, don't wait until you just happen to notice things. Be on the look out for them. Be ready for them. Plan in advance whenever possible. Remember, there should never be any competition between you and other motorists. The only challenge should be with yourself – to see how well you can comply with all that you have to do, with the emphasis on safety.

If you have still to sit the Driving Theory Test, I wish you success with it as well as your Practical Driving Test. If you are already past that stage I hope you enjoyed the book and I wish you safe driving.

INDEX

RIGHT WAY
PUBLISHING POLICY

HOW WE SELECT TITLES

RIGHT WAY consider carefully every deserving manuscript. Where an author is an authority on his subject but an inexperienced writer, we provide first-class editorial help. The standards we set make sure that every **RIGHT WAY** book is practical, easy to understand, concise, informative and delightful to read. Our specialist artists are skilled at creating simple illustrations which augment the text wherever necessary.

CONSISTENT QUALITY

At every reprint our books are updated where appropriate, giving our authors the opportunity to include new information.

FAST DELIVERY

We sell **RIGHT WAY** books to the best bookshops throughout the world. It may be that your bookseller has run out of stock of a particular title. If so, he can order more from us at any time – we have a fine reputation for "same day" despatch, and we supply any order, however small (even a single copy), to any bookseller who has an account with us. We prefer you to buy from your bookseller, as this reminds him of the strong underlying public demand for **RIGHT WAY** books. Readers who live in remote places, or who are housebound, or whose local bookseller is uncooperative, can order direct from us by post.

FREE

If you would like an up-to-date list of all **RIGHT WAY** titles currently available, please send a stamped self-addressed envelope to:

ELLIOT RIGHT WAY BOOKS,
KINGSWOOD, SURREY, KT20 6TD, U.K.

or visit our web site at www.right-way.co.uk